Edward Hayes Plumptre

The general Epistle of St. James

with notes and introduction

Edward Hayes Plumptre

The general Epistle of St. James
with notes and introduction

ISBN/EAN: 9783337728953

Printed in Europe, USA, Canada, Australia, Japan

Cover: Foto ©Lupo / pixelio.de

More available books at **www.hansebooks.com**

The Cambridge Bible for Schools and Colleges.

GENERAL EDITOR:—J. J. S. PEROWNE, D.D.,
DEAN OF PETERBOROUGH.

THE GENERAL EPISTLE OF

ST. JAMES,

WITH NOTES AND INTRODUCTION

BY

E. H. PLUMPTRE, D.D..
DEAN OF WELLS.

EDITED FOR THE SYNDICS OF THE UNIVERSITY PRESS.

Cambridge:
AT THE UNIVERSITY PRESS.
1890

PREFACE
BY THE GENERAL EDITOR.

THE General Editor of *The Cambridge Bible for Schools* thinks it right to say that he does not hold himself responsible either for the interpretation of particular passages which the Editors of the several Books have adopted, or for any opinion on points of doctrine that they may have expressed. In the New Testament more especially questions arise of the deepest theological import, on which the ablest and most conscientious interpreters have differed and always will differ. His aim has been in all such cases to leave each Contributor to the unfettered exercise of his own judgment, only taking care that mere controversy should as far as possible be avoided. He has contented himself chiefly with a careful revision of the notes, with pointing out omissions, with

PREFACE.

suggesting occasionally a reconsideration of some question, or a fuller treatment of difficult passages, and the like.

Beyond this he has not attempted to interfere, feeling it better that each Commentary should have its own individual character, and being convinced that freshness and variety of treatment are more than a compensation for any lack of uniformity in the Series.

DEANERY, PETERBOROUGH.

CONTENTS.

I. INTRODUCTION.   PAGES

    Chapter I. The Author of the Epistle ....   5—34

    Chapter II. To whom was the Epistle addressed   35—39

    Chapter III. The date of the Epistle ....   40—43

    Chapter IV. Analysis of the Epistle ....   43—45

II. TEXT AND NOTES ....   47—107

INTRODUCTION.

CHAPTER I.

THE AUTHOR OF THE EPISTLE.

I. THE name of *Jacôbus* or *Jacob*—which, after passing through various chances and changes of form, Spanish *Iago* and Portuguese *Xayme* (pronounced *Hayme*) and Italian *Giacomo* and French *Jacques* and *Jamè*, and Scotch *Hamish*, has at last dwindled into our monosyllabic *James*—was naturally, as having been borne by the great Patriarch whom Israel claimed as its progenitor, a favourite name among the later Jews[1]. In the New Testament we find two, or possibly three, persons who bore it: (1) James the son of Zebedee. (2) James the son of Alphæus. Both of these appear in all the lists of the Twelve Apostles. (3) There is a James described as the son of a Mary and the brother of a Joses or Joseph (Matt. xxvii. 56, Mark xv. 40), and a comparison of that passage with John xix. 25, defines this Mary as the wife of *Clôpas* (not *Cleophas* as in the English Version) and possibly also (though the construction is not free from ambiguity) as the sister of our Lord's mother. To his name is attached the epithet, not of "the less" as in the English version, as though it indicated difference in age or position, but of the "little," as an

---

[1] It is not without a feeling of regret, that I adopt in this volume the form in which the historical associations of the name have entirely disappeared. Usage, however, in such a matter, must be accepted as the *jus et norma loquendi*.

epithet descriptive in his case, as in that of Zacchæus (Luke xix. 3), of his stature. (4) There is a James whose name appears, together with Joses and Simon and Judas, in the lists of the "brethren" of the Lord, in Matt. xiii. 55, Mark vi. 3, and who is so described by St Paul in Gal. i. 19. St Paul's way of speaking of him there and in Gal. ii. 9, 12, leaves not a shadow of doubt as to the identity of this James with the one who occupies so prominent a position in the Church at Jerusalem in Acts xii. 17, xv. 13, xxi. 18.

The Epistle of St James may have been written, as far as the description which the writer gives of himself is concerned, by any one of these four, reserving the question whether the descriptions connected with (2), (3) and (4) give us any grounds for believing that the three accounts refer to two or even to one person only.

II. The hypothesis that the son of Zebedee, the brother of the beloved disciple, was the writer of the Epistle, has commonly been dismissed as hardly calling for serious consideration. It is not, however, without a certain amount of external authority, and has recently been maintained with considerable ability by the Rev. F. T. Bassett in a Commentary on the Epistle (Bagsters, 1876). It may be well therefore to begin with an inquiry into the grounds on which it rests.

(1) The oldest MSS. of the earlier, or Peshito, Syriac version, ranging from the 5th to the 8th century, state, in the superscription or subscription of the Epistle, or both, that it is an Epistle "of James the Apostle." Printed editions of the Syriac Version state more definitely that the three Epistles (James, 1 Peter, and 1 John) which that version includes, were written by the three Apostles who were witnesses of the Transfiguration, but it is uncertain on what MS. authority the statement was made. As far then as this evidence goes, it is of little or no weight in determining the authorship. It does not go higher than the fifth century, and leaves it an open question whether "James the Apostle" was the son of Zebedee, or the son of Alphæus, or the brother of the Lord, considered as having been raised to the office and title of an Apostle.

INTRODUCTION. 7

(2) A Latin MS. of the New Testament, giving a version of the Epistle prior to that of Jerome, states more definitely that it was written by "James the son of Zebedee," but the MS. is not assigned to an earlier date than the ninth century, and is therefore of little or no weight as an authority. Neither this nor the Syriac version can be looked on as giving more than the conjecture of the transcriber, or, at the best, a comparatively late and uncertain tradition.

(3) Admitting the weakness of the external evidence, Mr Bassett rests his case mainly on internal. It was, he thinks, *à priori* improbable that one who occupied so prominent a place among the Apostles during our Lord's ministry, whose name as one of the "Sons of Thunder" (Mark iii. 17) indicates conspicuous energy, should have passed away without leaving any written memorial for the permanent instruction of the Church. It is obvious, however, that all *à priori* arguments of this nature are, in the highest degree, precarious in their character, and that their only value lies in preparing the way for evidence of another kind.

(4) The internal coincidences on which Mr Bassett next lays stress are in themselves so suggestive and instructive, even if we do not admit his inference from them, that it seems worth while to state them briefly.

(*a*) There is, he points out, a strong resemblance between the teaching of the Epistle and that of John the Baptist, as is seen, e. g., in comparing

James i. 22, 27 with Matt. iii. 8
...... ii. 15, 16 ... Luke iii. 11
...... ii. 19, 20 ... Matt. iii. 9
...... v. 1—6 ... Matt. iii. 10—12.

And he infers from this the probability that the writer had been one of those who, like Peter, John and Andrew, had listened to the preaching of the Baptist.

(*b*) There are the frequently recurring parallelisms between the Epistle and the Sermon on the Mount, which strike the attention of well-nigh every reader.

James i. 2 compared with	Matt. v. 10—12
...... i. 4	v. 48
...... i. 5, v. 15	vii. 7—12
...... i. 9	v. 3
...... i. 20	v. 22
...... ii. 13	vi. 14, 15, v. 7
...... ii. 14	vii. 21—23
...... iii. 17, 18	v. 9
...... iv. 4	vi. 24
...... iv. 10	v. 3, 4
...... iv. 11	vii. 1—5
...... v. 2	vi. 19
...... v. 10	v. 12
...... v. 12	v. 33—37.

It is urged that the son of Zebedee was certainly among our Lord's disciples at the time the Sermon on the Mount was delivered, while there is no evidence that the son of Alphæus had as yet been called, and a distinct statement, assuming the brother of the Lord not to be identical with the son of Alphæus, that he at this time did not believe in Jesus as the Christ. (John vii. 5.)

(*c*) The writer finds in St James's description of Jesus as "the Lord of Glory" a reference, parallel to those of 2 Pet. i. 16—18 and John i. 14, to the vision on the Mount of Transfiguration which had been witnessed by Peter and the two sons of Zebedee.

(*d*) In the emphasis with which the writer of the Epistle condemns the sins of vainglory and rivalry and self-seeking ambition Mr Bassett finds a reference to the disputes and jealousies which during our Lord's ministry disturbed the harmony of the Apostolic company (comp. ch. i. 9—12, iii. 14—16 with Matt. xviii. 1, Mark ix. 34); in his protests against the "wrath of man" (ch. i. 19, 20), a reminiscence of his own passionate desire to call down fire from heaven, as Elijah had done of old (Luke ix. 54). With this and with Elijah's loss of patience (1 Kings xix. 4—10), he connects the statement that "Elias was a man of like passions with ourselves" (ch. v. 17).

(*e*) Stress is laid on the language of the Epistle as to the "coming of the Lord" as agreeing with what our Lord had said on the Mount of Olives in the hearing of the sons of Zebedee and of Jona (Mark xiii. 3). Compare

```
James ii. 6, 7  with Mark xiii. 9
 ...... iv. 1        ...  Mark xiii. 7
 ...... iv. 13, 14 ... Mark xiii. 32
 ...... v. 9         ...  Mark xiii. 29
 ...... v. 7         ...  Matt. xxiv. 27.
```

It is inferred that here also he was reproducing what he had himself heard.

(*f*) The not unfrequent parallelisms between this Epistle and 1 Peter are next brought to bear on the question. They are given as follows:—

```
James i. 2  with 1 Pet. i. 6—9
 ...... i. 10   ............ i. 24
 ...... i. 21   ............ ii. 1
 ...... iv. 6, 10 ......... v. 5
 ...... v. 20   ............ iv. 8.
```

It is urged that these coincidences of thought and phrase are just what might be expected in those who like the son of Zebedee and the son of Jona had been friends and companions in the work of disciples and Apostles.

(5) Interesting and suggestive as each of these lines of thought beyond question is, the evidence does not appear, on the whole, to warrant the conclusion which has been drawn from it. It would be a sufficient explanation of (*a*) and (*b*) that the writer of the Epistle had been *one* of the hearers of the Baptist and of our Lord, or had read or heard what we find recorded in St Matthew's Gospel. Of (*c*) it must be said that the epithet "of glory" was far too common (Acts vii. 2; Eph. i. 17; Col. i. 27; Heb. i. 3, ix. 5) to prove what it is alleged to prove. The faults mentioned under (*d*) were too much the besetting sins of the whole people to sustain any conclusion based on the supposition that they applied specially to the writer. It is obvious that the teaching of our Lord as to His "Coming," under (*e*), must, from a very early period, have become, at least to the extent to which the Epistle deals with it, the common property of all believers. Lastly, as to the parallelisms of (*f*) it must be

remembered that there is as much evidence that another James was for many years in constant communication with St Peter, as there is for the earlier friendship of that Apostle with the son of Zebedee.

On the whole, then, it is believed that this hypothesis, interesting and ingenious as it is, must be dismissed as not proven.

III. The name of the second Apostle who bore the name of James comes next under consideration. Can we think of the son of Alphæus as the writer of the Epistle? Here a preliminary question meets us : Are we to think of the son of Alphæus as identical with the brother of the Lord, and with "James the little," the son of Mary, the wife of Clôpas, and the sister of our Lord's mother? The view that one and the self-same person is described in these different ways has been so widely held that it is necessary to examine the grounds on which it rests.

(*a*) It has been supposed that Clôpas in John xix. 25 is another form, somewhat nearer to the Hebrew (*Chalpi*), of the name which is represented in the first three Gospels by Alphæus. This is in itself probable enough, but it is a question whether the same person would have been likely to have been known by both forms of the name in the same company of the disciples. The natural tendency, where the same names abound in any district, is that the men who bear them become known by distinct forms, or by epithets attached. *Primâ facie*, therefore, we should expect to find the Alphæus, who is the father of Levi or Matthew and of James, and possibly of the Judas who is connected with James in the list of the Twelve, a different person from Clôpas. There is at any rate far more ground for assuming the identity of the father of Matthew with the father of James (the name being the same in each case) than for looking on the two as distinct persons, and the latter as the same as Clôpas.

(*b*) The inference is, it is supposed, strengthened by the fact that Mary the wife of Clôpas is apparently identical with "Mary the *mother* of Joses" (Mark xv. 47) and of James (Mark xvi. 1, Luke xxiv. 10), of James the *little* and of Joses (Mark xv. 40), and that these two names appear in conjunction with Judas in the list of the brethren of the Lord (Mark vi. 3). It is assumed that the words of John xix. 25 refer the terms "his mother's sister" and "Mary the wife of Clôpas" to the same person, and that the James and Joses who were her sons were identical with the two who bear those names in the list of the four "brethren" of the Lord in Matt. xiii. 55, Mark vi. 3, and that they are called "brethren," though really only cousins.

Against this conclusion however we have to set the facts: (1) that it is by no means certain that in St John's enumeration of the women who stood by the Cross, "his mother, and his mother's sister, Mary the wife of Clôpas, and Mary Magdalene," even when taken by itself, warrants the inference that "his mother's sister" was identical with "the wife of Clôpas;" and (2) that a comparison with Matt. xxvii. 56, and Mark xv. 40, makes it far more probable that she was the same as Salome, the mother of the sons of Zebedee. (3) In Acts i. 13, the "brethren" are named after the Eleven Apostles, and clearly as distinct from them; St Paul, in 1 Cor. ix. 5, in like manner distinguishes them from the Apostles. It is *primâ facie* utterly improbable that the two writers should so have spoken had three, or even two, of the "brethren" been enrolled in the company of the Twelve. (4) Yet more important in its bearing on the question is the part taken by the "brethren of the Lord" throughout His ministry. They come, with the mother of Jesus, to check His preaching, and are contrasted by Him with His disciples as His true brethren (Matt. xii. 46—50; Mark iii. 31—35; Luke viii. 19—21). The tone in which the men of Nazareth speak of them (Matt. xiii. 55; Mark vi. 3) is hardly compatible with the thought that they had accepted Him as the Christ. As late as the last Feast of Tabernacles before the Crucifixion, St John definitely quotes words as spoken by them which imply doubt and distrust, and states that they did not then believe on Him (John vii. 5). It is surely scarcely conceivable that those of whom such things are said could have been among the Twelve who were sent forth to proclaim their Lord as the Head of the Divine Kingdom. On these grounds, therefore, in spite of the authority of many great names which might be cited in its favour, we are, I believe, compelled to reject the hypothesis that James the son of

Alphæus was identical with the brother of the Lord, and except on that hypothesis, there are absolutely no grounds whatever, external or internal, to connect the former with the authorship of this Epistle.

IV. It remains, therefore, that we should (1) consider the claims of the last-named James, known as the brother of the Lord, and (2) inquire into the nature of the relationship which that name was intended to express. When these two points are settled we can pass on, without further hindrance, to what we know of the life and character of the writer.

It must be admitted that the evidence in this case begins at a comparatively late date. Eusebius (*Hist.* III. 25, circ. A.D. 330) reckons "the Epistle known as James's" among the writings which, though accepted by the majority, were yet open to question (*antilegomena*). It is clear from another passage that by this James, the reputed author of the Epistle, he means "the brother of the Lord," to whom the Apostles had assigned the "throne" of the bishopric of Jerusalem (*Hist.* II. 23). The first of the Epistles known as Catholic was said to be his. He adds, however, in his truthful desire of accuracy, "It should be known that it is counted spurious by some. Not many of the ancients, at any rate, have made mention of it, as neither have they of that of Judas, which also is one of the seven Catholic Epistles. But nevertheless we know that these two have been publicly read and received in very many Churches." Origen (*Comm. in Joann.* xix. 6) had spoken of "the Epistle reputed to be by James," and quotes from it as by him (*Hom.* VIII. *in Exod.*), but does not specify to which James he assigns it. Jerome, whose long residence at Bethlehem makes him the representative of the Syrian as well as the Western tradition, takes up the language of Eusebius. "James who is called the brother of the Lord, known also as the Just, wrote one Epistle only, which is one of the seven Catholic Epistles. Yet that too is said to have been set forth by some one else in his name, though gradually, as time went on, it gained authority." (*Catalog. Script. Eccles.*)

The very early list of the books of the New Testament, in the Ambrosian Library at Milan, known, from the name of its first editor, as the Muratorian Fragment, and referred to a date about A.D. 190, though having no authority, except from its antiquity, is remarkable as confirming the statement of Eusebius that the Epistle of St James was not universally accepted. The list includes, besides books about which there was no doubt, the Epistle of Jude, and two Epistles of St John, the Apocalypse of Peter (a book conspicuously apocryphal), the *Shepherd* of Hermas, and even the *Wisdom of Solomon*, but it makes no mention of the Epistle of St James. After the time of Eusebius, however, in spite of the doubting tone in which he speaks, it won its way to general acceptance. It appears in the list of the Council of Laodicea, c. 59 (A.D. 363), of the third Council of Carthage, c. 39 (A.D. 397), of the so-called Apostolic Canons. It is acknowledged by Cyril of Jerusalem (*Catech.* IV. 33, A.D. 349), by Epiphanius of Cyprus (*Adv. hær.* LXXVI. 5, circ. A.D. 403), by Athanasius (*Epist. Test.* 39, before A.D. 373), by Gregory of Nazianzus (A.D. 391), and no question was raised as to its authority till the 16th century, when the dogmatic bias of Luther and his school led them to revive the old doubts as to its inspiration and canonicity.

The conclusion from these facts would seem to be that the Epistle of St James came somewhat slowly into general circulation. It was natural that it should do so. Though addressed to the Twelve Tribes of the Dispersion, it does not follow that any very effectual measures were taken to secure its reaching them. And so far as copies did find their way to distant cities, they were addressed, we must remember, to the declining and decaying party of the Church of the Circumcision. They came from one whose name had been identified, rightly or wrongly, with that party in its attitude of antagonism to the teaching of St Paul and the freedom of the Gentile Churches. The writer's personal influence had not extended beyond the Churches of Judea, and the Churches of the Gentiles did not feel the impression made on those who knew him by the saintliness of his life and character. The writer of the Muratorian Fragment represents this early stage of the history of the Epistle. He does not reject it. He has obviously not heard of it. When the letter becomes known to the students and scholars of the Church, to men like Origen, Eusebius and Jerome, they naturally at first speak of it with some hesitation. After a time inquiry leads to a more prompt and unquestioning acceptance. The more critical writers have no doubt that the James, whose name it bears, was the brother of the Lord, and not the son of Zebedee; and their judgment, as the result of inquiry and given in the teeth of the natural tendency to claim an Apostolic authority for any fragment of the Apostolic age, may well be looked on as outweighing the conjecture of a Syrian transcriber in the 9th century who yielded to that tendency, or the scarcely less conjectural inferences of recent writers.

V. So far, then, we have reached a fairly firm standing ground, and may take a fresh start on the assumption that the Epistle was written, not by the son of Zebedee, nor by the son of Alphæus, but by James the brother of the Lord. A question of great difficulty, however, once more meets us on the threshold. What kind of relationship did that description imply? Very different answers have been given to that question.

(1) We have the view that the "brethren of the Lord" were the sons of Joseph and of Mary, and therefore His younger brothers. This has in its favour, the common and natural, though not, it must be admitted, the necessary, meaning of the Greek word for "brethren," perhaps, also, the *primâ facie* inference from Matt. i. 25. It was adopted by Helvidius, a Latin writer of the 4th century, and has been revived by some recent scholars of high reputation, among whom are Dean Alford and Canon Farrar. It has against it the general *consensus* of the Fathers of the third and fourth century, resting on a wide-spread belief in the perpetual virginity of the mother of the Lord, and the fact that Helvidius was treated as propounding a new and monstrous theory. It may be admitted that the word does not necessarily mean that those who bore it were children of the same mother, and that Matt. i. 25 does not necessarily imply what, at first sight, it appears to mean. It is scarcely likely, however, with such words at hand as the Greek for "sister's son" (Col. iv. 10) or "cousins" (Luke i. 36), that it

would have been used to express either of those relationships. Slightly weighing against it, perhaps, are (1) the action and tone of the brethren in relation to our Lord (Matt. xii. 46; John vii. 3—5), which is that of elder rather than younger relatives, and (2) the fact that the mother of our Lord is commended to the care of John, the son of Zebedee and Salome (John xix. 26), and not to those who, on this view, would have been her more natural protectors. It is probable, however, as stated above, that the wife of Zebedee may have been the sister of the Virgin, and if so, then there were close ties of relationship uniting St John to the latter. All that can be said is that the New Testament writers, if their language does not exclude the alternative theories, are, at least, not in any measure careful to exclude this.

(2) There is the theory that the "brethren" were the children of Joseph by a former marriage. It need scarcely be said that there is nothing in the New Testament to prove such a theory. Indirectly it falls in with what has just been said as to their tone towards our Lord, and the preference of a sister's son (assuming Salome to have been the "mother's sister" of John xix. 25) to step-sons as a guardian and protector, would be sufficiently in harmony with the practices of common life. In the second, third, and fourth centuries this appears to have been the favourite view. It met the reverential feeling which, rightly or wrongly, shrank from the thought that the wedded life of the mother of Jesus was like that of other women. It gave to the word "brethren," without any violence, an adequate or natural meaning. It was maintained by Epiphanius (A.D. 367), by Origen (*in Joann.* ii. 12, *in Matt.* xiii. 55), Eusebius (*Hist.* II. 1), Hilary of Poitiers (A.D. 368), Gregory of Nyssa (A.D. 394), Cyril of Alexandria (*in Gen.* vii. p. 221), and with the modification that Joseph's first marriage was with the widow of his brother Clôpas, by Theophylact (Comm. on Matt. xiii. 55, Gal. i. 19). It has been revived in our own time by Canon Lightfoot (*Excursus* on "The brethren of the Lord" in *Commentary on Galatians*), and maintained as against the third hypothesis now to be mentioned, with arguments which seem to the present writer to admit of no satisfactory answer.

(3) Lastly, there is the theory already alluded to, that the "brethren" were the sons of the wife of Clôpas, who is identified with the sister of the Virgin, and that they were thus called "brethren" in the wider sense in which that word may be used of "cousins." Clôpas is held (though this was an afterthought of writers later than Jerome, who was the first to propound this view) to be identical with Alphæus, and James the brother of the Lord is held to be identical with James the son of Alphæus, in the list of the Apostles, and "Jude *of James*" to be another of the brethren, and Simon, a third brother, is identified with Simon Zelotes, or the Canaanite. The theory was first started by Jerome (*Catal. Vir. Illustr.; Adv. Helvid.*)[1] in his eagerness to vindicate the perpetual virginity of Mary against what seemed to him the heresy of Helvidius, but though maintained vehemently at first, was afterwards treated by him as a matter of comparative indifference (Lightfoot's *Excursus, ut supra*). His influence, however, gave currency to the theory in the Western Church, and it was probably received by Ambrose (whose language, however, is consistent with the Epiphanian theory) in his treatise *De Institutione Virginis*, and by Augustine (*in Joann.* XXVIII., *Enarr.* in Ps. cxxvii., *Contr. Faust.* XXII. 35). The Western Church, accordingly, in her Calendar has recognised only two Saints of the name of James, and has naturally been followed in this respect by the Church of England, which gives July 25 to the son of Zebedee, and May 1st to St Philip and the son of Alphæus. The choice of the Epistle for that day implies his identification with the brother of the Lord. In the Greek Church, on the other hand, we trace, beyond the shadow of doubt, the survival of the Epiphanian view, or perhaps of the still older tradition on which it rested, Oct. 9th being dedicated

---

[1] Dr Mill (*Mythical Interp.* p. 291) quotes a passage from a MS. of the 14th century, ascribed to Papias, and maintaining Jerome's view as proof of an almost apostolic antiquity for this theory. The occurrence of the mediæval " Star of the Sea," as applied to the Virgin, is, however, in itself proof of a much later date than that of Papias of Hierapolis, and Dr Lightfoot shews that it comes from a work by a writer of the same name in the 11th century.

INTRODUCTION.   17

to the son of Alphæus, and Oct. 23rd to the brother of the Lord. It is not probable, looking to the language of the Greek Church as to the Virgin, that this distinction between the two whom writers that follow the Roman view identify, rests on its acceptance of the Helvidian view.

On the whole, then, in a question confessedly of considerable difficulty, we may rest in the conclusions :

(1) That there is absolutely no ground for identifying James the brother of the Lord with the son of Alphæus, and therefore none for believing him to have been of the number of the Twelve Apostles.

(2) That there is absolutely no ground for believing the brethren of the Lord to have been the children of the Virgin's sister, and therefore only cousins.

(3) That the first impression made by the language of the New Testament is in favour of their being brethren in the fullest sense of the word, but that this language is not incompatible with the view that they were the children of Joseph by a previous marriage.

VI. I have been reluctant up to this point to bring in the evidence of apocryphal or spurious writings. But it will be admitted, assuming the above conclusions as at least partly proved, that it is an enquiry not without interest to ask what relation the narratives of such writings bear to them.

In the *Protevangelium Jacobi*, an apocryphal narrative, dating probably from the second century, and therefore prior to any of the theories which originated in the fourth, Joseph appears as an old man with sons at the time of his espousals (c. 9), but with no daughter (c. 17). The sons are with him at Bethlehem at the time of the Nativity. James himself is represented as writing the book after the death of Herod the Great (c. 25). The *Gospel of the Pseudo-Matthew* agrees as to the age of Joseph (c. 8), and relates that James, "the first-born son of Joseph," was bitten in the hand by a viper in his boyhood, and was healed by the touch and the breath of Jesus (c. 31). Joseph, Judas, and Simeon are named as the other brothers. Anna, the mother of the Virgin, after the death of her first husband,

Joachim, marries Cleophas, and has by him a second daughter Mary, who in her turn is married to Alphæus, and becomes the mother of Philip and James, the Apostles. The *History of Joseph* (c. 3) gives the names of the four sons, and Assia and Lydia as the names of the daughters, and relates that Joseph became a widower when Mary was of the age of twelve, lived to the age of 111, James and Judas remaining in the household till his death (c. 14), and died with Jesus holding his hands, and receiving his last sigh (c. 19). The *Gospel of Thomas* repeats the story of the viper that bit James (c. 16). The Arabic *Gospel of the Infancy* makes James and Joses grown up while Jesus is yet an infant.

The Apocryphal Gospels thus referred to are so full of frivolous and fantastic fables, that no single fact narrated in them can claim, on that ground, the slightest degree of credibility; but the uniform consent of so many books written in various languages and countries, in adopting the Epiphanian view as distinct alike from that of Helvidius and that of Jerome, must be admitted as shewing what was in the second and third centuries the current tradition of the Church. It was not probable that writers aiming at attracting popular admiration would run counter to any prevalent tradition that "the brethren of the Lord" were really only His cousins.

VII. Leaving the region of legends, but keeping on the stratum of truth which underlies them, we may venture to picture to ourselves that household of Nazareth in at least the outline of its life. We can think of the elder brothers watching with loving admiration the growth of the Holy Child that "increased in wisdom and in stature and in favour with God and man." Their training had been after the pattern of that which prevailed in all devout Jewish houses. They had known the Holy Scriptures daily. They heard it read in the Synagogue on the Sabbath day. They read it in their home. But in that village of Nazareth, as throughout Galilee, Greek was probably both spoken and read familiarly, and thus they might become acquainted with the teaching of books which the Alexandrian Jews had added to the Hebrew Canon. Their father dies, and then they marry (1 Cor. ix. 5), and, it may well have been, leave their step-mother to be maintained by the younger Half-Brother who was her own son. So the years pass on till the preaching of the Baptist breaks through the orderly routine with the energy of a new force. The brothers go from Nazareth as others go from Capernaum, and James learns the lessons which he afterwards reproduces in his Epistle, and adopts the Nazarite rule, for the rigorous observance of which his life was afterwards conspicuous. And then follows that which to him, as to the other dwellers in Nazareth, was a marvel and a stumblingblock. The younger Brother proclaims in the Synagogue, probably on the great Day of Atonement, that the most glorious promises of the Prophets, which were read on that day as the appointed lesson, were fulfilled in Him. They have loved and honoured Him up to this time, but they are not prepared for this. They fear the probable effects of such a proclamation in raising the opposition of Pharisees and Scribes or the jealous suspicion of the Tetrarch Antipas. They hold back from joining the company of the disciples. The oft-repeated words of Jesus, that "a prophet is not without honour but in his own country, and among his own kin, and in his own house" (Mark vi. 4; Matt. xiii. 57; Luke iv. 24; John iv. 44), are spoken as with a plaintive reference to a definite personal experience. They, too, are tempted to take up the half-taunting words, "Physician, heal thyself," and to demand that wonders as great as those of which they had heard at Capernaum should be wrought in their presence in their own city. They hear a few months afterwards that the Mission of the Kingdom is going on at Jerusalem and throughout Galilee, that Scribes and Pharisees have come down from Jerusalem to watch, and, if possible, to entrap the new Teacher (Luke v. 17), that they have coalesced with the Herodians against Him, and are plotting against His life (Mark iii. 6). They and His mother are anxious to protect Him against that danger. And so they leave Nazareth, and appear on the outskirts of the crowd at Capernaum at the very moment when the antagonism was becoming more and more embittered, and the situation more full of danger (Matt. xii. 46). They are anxious to utter their words of warning, to restrain Him, while there is yet time, from irrevocable words which may lead to a shameful death. They hear in return the declaration, so full of blessing for others, so full of warning and reproof for them, "Behold my mother and my brethren! For whosoever shall do the will of my Father which is in Heaven, the same is my brother and sister and mother" (Matt. xii. 49, 50). So far their efforts were frustrated; but the heart of the Brother yearns over the kindred and the neighbours who were so slow of heart to believe, and He appears once again in the Synagogue of Nazareth (Matt. xiii. 54—58). The brothers listen, admiring but still not believing, and the men of Nazareth appeal, as it were, to their self-esteem. What was He in outward birth or condition, that He should be more than they? "Is not this the carpenter's son, Himself a carpenter? Is not His mother called Mary? Are not His brethren, James and Joses and Simon and Judas, with us?" (Matt. xiii. 55; Mark vi. 3). Once again the old sad proverb was fulfilled, and He of whom these things were said could do but few works of power there because of their unbelief (Mark vi. 5).

The months passed on apparently with little or no change of feeling. The Feast of Tabernacles came, the last that preceded the Passion, and the brethren were going up with other Galilæans to the Holy City. They turned to the Prophet in whom they did not as yet believe with the measure of belief which He required, in a tone of impatient expectation, Why remain in Galilee if He were indeed the King of Israel? "Depart hence, and go into Judæa, that thy disciples also"—obviously the disciples in Jerusalem, of whom they had heard as listening to Him in his previous visits—"may see the works that thou doest. For there is no man that doeth any thing in secret, and he himself seeketh to be known openly" (John vii. 3—5). "If thou do these things," if thou canst heal the sick and give sight to the blind and cast out devils, "shew thyself to the world," to that world of which they thought as gathering in Jerusalem to keep the coming Feast. That challenge He did not accept, for it implied that they, and not He, were judges as to the time and manner of His Manifestation. Their time was "always ready," but His was mapped out for Him by a Wisdom higher than theirs, and His time was not yet full come (John vii. 8). They, we know, were present at the Feast, and they found the thoughts of the men of Judæa concerning Him fluctuating and uncertain. Some acknowledged Him as the Prophet, some as the Christ, some spoke of Him as a deceiver (John vii. 40, 41, 47). Attempts were made to seize Him, and made in vain. The Feast ended as it began, in division, and the last words which they may have heard were, "He hath a devil and is mad"—words which might almost seem to have been an echo of their own thoughts, when they, or those whom they had sent, said "He is beside Himself" (Mark iii. 21).

The last Passover came, and the brethren, we must believe, were there, with the others who came from Galilee. Perhaps they too thought that the long-delayed manifestation for which they had craved was at last to be granted, and that "the kingdom of God was to immediately appear" (Luke xix. 11). But it is significant that He eats the Passover, which was essentially the religious feast of the *family*, not with them, as would, under common conditions, have been natural, but with the Twelve, to whom He had pointed as being His true brethren. Then came what would seem to them the fulfilment of all their worst forebodings, the capture, the condemnation, and the death. It may be inferred from John xix. 26 that it was the beloved disciple, the nephew, and not the step-son, of the Mother of the Lord, who accompanied her to the place of Crucifixion, but they too could hardly have been absent from that awful spectacle. And then came that which changed their doubt and hesitation into faith. The risen Lord was seen of Cephas and of the Twelve, and then of five hundred brethren at once, and after that, of James (1 Cor. xv. 5—7). When St Paul thus wrote, the one person of whom his readers would think as thus referred to, was neither the son of Zebedee, who was no longer among the living witnesses of the Resurrection, nor the son of Alphæus, who was to the Corinthians, as to us, hardly more than a name. He could refer, they would say, to none other than the brother of the Lord, whom they knew as the Bishop of Jerusalem, the head of the Church of the Circumcision. A legend or tradition in the *Gospel according to the Hebrews*, which takes its place among the more respectable of the New Testament Apocrypha, and was translated by Jerome himself into both Greek and Latin, connects this appearance with an incident sufficiently suggestive to be worth inserting here. James had sworn, we are told, that he would not eat bread from the hour in which he had drunk of the Lord's cup until he should see Him rising from the dead. "And the Lord went and appeared to him, and said after a while, Bring hither a table and set bread on it ; and He took bread and blessed it, and brake it, and gave it to James the Just, and said to him, My brother, eat thy bread now, for the Son of Man hath risen from among those that sleep." (Jerome, *Catal. Script. Eccles.*). The narrative presents, it is obvious, so many analogies with other manifestations recorded in the Gospels, that admitting the fact of the appearance to James, on the strength of St Paul's statement, this may well be received as giving what was probably the manner.

Some such appearance, at any rate, offers the only reasonable explanation of the next fact in the life of St James recorded in the New Testament. The Resurrection and the Ascension are passed, and the "brethren" are with the Twelve in the Upper Chamber in Jerusalem (Acts i. 14). They take part in the election of Matthias, and are sharers in the marvellous gifts of the Spirit on the Day of Pentecost (Acts ii. 1—4). From that time they cast in their lot with the fortunes of the infant Church, and their earthly relationship to the Lord of that Church, the witness they were able to bear to the blameless Youth and Manhood at Nazareth, no less than to the fact of the Resurrection, must have given them a marked prominence in the company of the disciples. They accepted the admission of the Samaritans into the infant Church. On St Paul's return to Jerusalem, three years after his conversion, he was received by Peter alone of the Apostles, and by James the Lord's brother (Gal. i. 18, 19)[1]. It seems probable that on the death

[1] It has sometimes been inferred from St Paul's way of speaking ("other of the Apostles saw I none save James the Lord's brother") that the one so named must have been among the Twelve, and therefore

of James the brother of John, his namesake, the brother of the Lord, succeeded, either by direct election, or by tacit acceptance, into the place thus left vacant. When the persecution under Agrippa made it necessary for Peter to leave Jerusalem, the language of the Apostle on his departure implies that James was left as the guide and teacher of the Church (Acts xii. 17). It may fairly be assumed that he was among the elders who received the alms that had been collected by the Gentile converts at Antioch (Acts xi. 30) for the disciples at Jerusalem. We may reasonably trace an allusion to that act of benevolence, and to the new name of Christians which had been applied to the disciples at Antioch (Acts xi. 26), in the language of the Epistle (see Notes on ch. ii. 7, 16). It was, probably, one of the consequences of the new position which he thus occupied, that in view of the expansion of the Church, he wrote his Encyclical Epistle to the twelve tribes of the Dispersion, addressing primarily those among them that had embraced the faith of the Lord Jesus Christ (ch. i. 1, ii. 1, v. 7), but indirectly calling all the families of Israel to repentance, and faith, and holiness (see *Introduction* ch. ii.). Then, after seventeen years had passed since the conversion of St Paul, we find him presiding at the Council of Jerusalem, recognised as, by age and position, the representative of the Church of the Circumcision (Acts xv. 13). The devotion, purity, asceticism of his life, his faithfulness and loving observance of all rules which devout Pharisees practised, had won for him the respect of that party as a whole. It was not strange, perhaps, that those of its members who had accepted the faith of Christ should look upon him as their ideal Apostle, and present his life to the Gentile converts as the example which they were bound to follow. He, they seem to have said, would never sanction the baptism of uncircumcised proselytes as members of the Church of Christ, nor their exemption from the rules of the Law and the traditions of the Elders. He, on his part, however, disclaims that inference from his conduct.

identical with the son of Alphæus. The examples of a like construction in Luke iv. 26, 27 shew that no such inference is reliable. The woman of Sarepta was not one of the widows of Israel, nor was Naaman one of its lepers.

He had given no such commandment (Acts xv. 24). He had learnt from the Prophet whose teaching he reproduces (comp. Amos viii. 5, 10 with James iv. 13, v. 1, 2; Amos vi. 1—6 with James v. 5), in whom he found a Nazarite like himself (Amos ii. 11, 12), to welcome the conversion of the "residue of men," and to receive as brethren all "the Gentiles upon whom the name of the Lord is called" (Acts xv. 17). He suggests as the right solution of the immediate problem, that the Gentile Christians should be received on the footing which the more liberal Pharisees had accepted as that of the Proselytes of the Gate, bound to the precepts of Noah, but not to those of Moses (Acts xv. 20). He gives to Paul and Barnabas the right hand of fellowship (Gal. ii. 9), accepts in full the Gospel which they had preached (Acts xv. 25, 26), and publicly gives his sanction to the work they had done among the Gentiles. He recognises in so doing that the Law which he himself continued to observe with so much rigour, might be to others a yoke not easy and a burden not light (Matt. xi. 29, 30), and that the only law of liberty was the law of the true King, "Thou shalt love thy neighbour as thyself" (Acts xv. 10, 19; James i. 25, ii. 8).

It is scarcely likely that, after this frank and full acceptance, attested not by St Luke only, but by St Paul himself, in the Epistle in which he is most eager to vindicate his entire independence of the Church at Jerusalem, St James would have taken up the position of antagonism which some recent writers assign to him in the history of the Apostolic Church, which they have constructed out of their inner consciousness, resting on the assumption that the wild romances of the *Clementine Homilies* and *Recognitions* contain a more trustworthy history than the Acts of the Apostles. And the most natural explanation of the fact that St Peter's conduct at Antioch, in relation to the Gentiles, was altered for the worse when "certain came from James" (Gal. ii. 12), is that then, as before, his name was used by those to whom he had given no such commandment, to enforce their interpretation of the *Concordat* which had been adopted, on his proposal, at the Council of Jerusalem. It is clear at any rate, that, while on the one hand, his own life was such as to win the admiration of those who were most zealous for the Law, he still continued, on the other, to hold out to St Paul the right hand of fellowship. He must have received him on the occasion of the visit of which we have only the brief fragmentary record of Acts xviii. 22. He welcomes him, when he comes once again, accompanied by many Gentile converts, confirms the terms of the great Charter of Gentile freedom, and makes the characteristic suggestion that St Paul should shew that he himself "walked orderly and kept the Law," by doing partially, but as fully as circumstances admitted, what he had done more thoroughly before, and presenting himself in the Temple as one who had upon him the vow of the Nazarite (Acts xxi. 18—25). Here, as far as the New Testament is concerned, we take our leave of him, and have to depend on the less certain guidance of later history. A brief narrative of his death is found in Josephus (*Ant.* XX. 9 § 1), but it has been regarded by many writers as a Christian interpolation. It states that when Albinus succeeded Festus (Acts xxiv. 27) as Procurator of Judæa, the younger Ananus, or Annas (son of the High Priest so named in Luke iii. 2; John xviii. 13), was himself High Priest, bold and daring in character. He was of the sect of Sadducees (comp. Acts iv. 4, v. 17) who were always conspicuous for harshness in all judicial proceedings (comp. Joseph. *Ant.* XIII. 10 § 6, *Wars*, II. 8 § 14). And so, taking advantage of the interval between the death of Festus and the arrival of Albinus, he called together a Council of Judges (clearly the Sanhedrin), and "he brought before it the brother of Jesus that was called Christ, whose name was James, and certain others, and having charged them with transgressing the law, delivered them to be stoned. Some of the most equitable in the city, however, and those who were most accurate in their knowledge of the Law, were grieved at this. They sent secretly to the King (the Agrippa of Acts xxv. 13), begging him to restrain Ananus from such acts of violence. Some of them meet Albinus on his way from Alexandria, to tell him what Ananus had done, and how it was unlawful for him to convene the Council without his consent, and the result was that Albinus wrote him a threatening letter, and that Agrippa deposed him from the priesthood."

The story of his death is told in a more dramatic form, and probably with some legendary admixture, by Hegesippus, the historian of the Jews, who wrote in the third quarter of the second century. The passage (quoted by Euseb. *Hist.* II. 23) is so interesting, and in some respects so important, that it will be well to give it at length.

"James the brother of the Lord receives the Church from the Apostles, he who was called the Just from the Lord's time even to our own; for many bore the name of James. This man was holy from his mother's womb. He drank no wine nor strong drink, nor did he eat any thing that lives. No razor came upon his head, nor did he anoint himself with oil, nor use the bath. He only was allowed to enter into the holy place, for he wore no woollen, but linen garments only. And he was wont to go alone into the sanctuary, and used to be found prostrate on his knees, and asking forgiveness for the people, so that his knees grew hard and worn, like a camel's, because he was ever kneeling and worshipping God, and asking forgiveness for the people. And on account of his exceeding righteousness he was called the Righteous (or the Just), and Oblias, which means in Greek 'the bulwark of the people' and 'righteousness,' as the prophets shew of him. Some then of the seven sects of the people, of those whom I have described in my Memoirs, were wont to ask him, Who is the door of Jesus? And he was wont to say that this was the Saviour. And of these some believed that Jesus is the Christ. But the sects of which I have spoken did not believe either in the Resurrection, or in Him who cometh to give to every man according to his works. As many then as believed did so on account of James. And when many of the rulers also believed, there was a stir of the Jews and Scribes and Pharisees, saying that the whole people were in danger of looking for Jesus the Christ. They came together and said to James: 'We entreat thee, restrain the people, for they have gone astray to Jesus as though He were indeed the Christ. We beseech thee to persuade all that come to the day of the Passover concerning Jesus; for we all hearken to thee. For all of us bear thee witness, and all the people also, that thou art righteous, and art no respecter of persons. Do thou therefore persuade the multitude not to be led astray concerning Jesus; for we and all the people hearken unto thee. Stand therefore on the pinnacle of the Temple, that thou mayest be conspicuous aloft, and that thy words may easily be heard by all the people, for by reason of the Passover all the tribes have come together, and with them the Gentiles.' So the Scribes and Pharisees before-mentioned placed James on the pinnacle of the Temple, and they cried out to him, and said, 'O thou Righteous one, to whom we are all bound to hearken, since the people are all gone astray after Jesus that was crucified, tell us what is the door of Jesus.' And he answered with a loud voice: 'Why ask ye me concerning Jesus the Son of man? He hath sat down in Heaven on the right hand of the Great Power, and is about to come upon the clouds of Heaven.' And when many were fully persuaded, and were glorifying God for the testimony of James, and saying, 'Hosanna to the Son of David,' then again the same Scribes and Pharisees said one to another, 'We did ill in giving scope for such a testimony to Jesus, but let us go up and cast him down, that they may fear and not believe him.' And they cried out, saying, 'Ho, ho, even the Righteous is gone astray!' And they fulfilled the scripture that is written in Isaiah, Let us make away with the Righteous, for he is displeasing to us; therefore shall they eat of the fruit of their works. And they went and cast the Righteous one down; and they said one to another, 'Let us stone James the Righteous.' And they began to stone him, for when he was cast down he did not die at once, but turned and fell on his knees, saying, 'O Lord God our Father, forgive them, I beseech Thee, for they know not what they do.' And while they were thus stoning him, one of the priests of the sons of Rechab the son of Rechabim, of whom the Prophet Jeremiah bears record, cried out and said, 'Cease ye: what is it that ye are doing? The Righteous one is praying for you.' And one of them, who was a fuller, took the club wherewith he was wont to beat his clothes, and smote the head of the Righteous one with it. And so he bore his witness. And they buried him at the place beside the Sanctuary, and his tombstone remaineth by the Sanctuary. He was, and is, a true witness both to Jews and Greeks, that Jesus is the Christ."

There is but little, if anything, in this narrative, that is in itself improbable. The picture drawn of St James's life agrees with the position occupied by him in Acts xx. 23 as the centre of those who were all zealous of the Law, as giving prominence to the Nazarite vow as an act of devotion, as wishing above all things to stop the mouths of disputants and gainsayers. The long-continued prayer in the Temple is but the natural development of the teaching of the Epistle as to the power of effectual fervent prayer. The use of linen garments only was after the rule of the Essenes (Joseph. *Wars*, II. 8 § 4). The abstinence from wine and animal food was what might be expected in one who had been a student of the prophet who gave such prominence to the Nazarite vow (Amos ii. 11, 12; Acts xv. 16), who had been also a follower of the Baptist, and so largely reproduced his teaching. The non-use of the bath need not be understood of any neglect of the multiplied ablutions which were practised by all Pharisees and devout Jews, above all, by the Essenes (Joseph. *Wars*, II. 8 § 3), whose life approximated to the type presented by that of St James and of the Baptist. The "bath" in the language of the writers of that age was the Roman bath with its *sudatorium, frigidarium,* shampooing, and other appliances, which was naturally looked upon by those who were leading an ascetic life as an effeminate luxury. Even the more startling fact, that the brother of the Lord was allowed to enter into the Sanctuary, is not without a parallel (assuming the term to point not to the Holy of Holies, but to the Court of the Priests) in the privileges which were granted to other Nazarites, and which led a later Jewish writer (Maimonides, *More Nevochim* III. 43) to place those who took that vow on them as a life-long obligation, on a level with the High Priest; and the mention of the priest of the sons of Rechab, who naturally sympathised with one whose life

INTRODUCTION.

was like his own, is explained by the fact, sufficiently established by the Targum of Jonathan and other evidence (see *Dictionary of the Bible*, Art. "Rechabites"), that they were adopted, after the Captivity, into the tribe of Levi, perhaps into the family of Aaron, and became entitled to their privileges. The tradition reported by Epiphanius (*Hær.* 78) that he, like St John at Ephesus (*Eus.* v. 24), wore the πέταλον, or thin plate of gold, with the words "Holiness to the Lord," which belonged to the High Priest (Exod. xxviii. 36), represents, it is obvious, the same ideas, and in spite of its apparent strangeness, need not be rejected as in itself incredible[1]. The name Oblias[2], with the explanation which Hegesippus gives of it, represents the reverence felt by the population of Jerusalem for one who was to them the last surviving representative of the saintly life, and which shewed itself in their feeling that when he was murdered their defence was gone, and that the calamities that then followed in such quick succession were the just punishment of that deed of blood (Euseb. *Hist.* II. 23). The question which seems to us at first scarcely intelligible, What is the door of Jesus? connects itself with the teaching of the Epistle that "the Judge standeth at the *door*" (ch. v. 9). One who had those words often on his lips as a warning against the selfish luxury of the generation in which he lived, was likely enough to hear from Saducean priests, themselves foremost in that luxury, the mocking question,

---

[1] It may be noted, in connexion with this statement, that the portrait of Josephus, commonly found in the English editions, represents him with this *petalon*. I do not know from what picture the engraving was made, but the fact seems to indicate that the practice was not so strange as it appears to us. Josephus, it will be remembered, claimed descent from the sons of Aaron, and it is not unlikely that both St John and the brother of the Lord may have had a like claim (see Article "Priests" in the *Dictionary of the Bible*). Jerome, whose personal knowledge goes for something in such a matter, says that Josephus was in such favour with Vespasian and Titus, that he had a public statue at Rome (*Catal. Script. Illust.*), so that there may have been some authority in the fourth century for such a representation.

[2] The probable Hebrew form of the word was *Ophli-am* (=stronghold of the people), the first half of the word being identical with *Ophel*, the tower on the south side of the Temple, which was the residence of the Levites (Neh. xi. 21).

"What is that *door* of which we hear so much?" They did not hear anything, though the Judge was standing at the door and knocked.

VI. Later traditions present features that are either dimmer or more distorted. The party that had misrepresented St James in his life continued their work after he was dead; and in the controversial romance known as the *Homilies* of the Pseudo-Clement of Rome, Peter writes to the brother of the Lord, and maintains the perpetual obligation of the Law of Moses against the preaching of the man (obviously the forger of the letter means St Paul) who was "his enemy," and James delivers the record of his teaching to men who are at once "devout and circumcised and faithful," and binds them by a solemn oath, like that of the Freemasons or other secret societies, to absolute secresy and obedience (*Epistle of Peter, prefixed to the Clementine Homilies*). The Pseudo-Clement dedicates his work to "his lord James, the bishop of bishops, who rules Jerusalem, the Holy Church of the Hebrews" (*Epist. of Clement*). In a second romance known as the *Recognitions*, ascribed to the same writer, St James, the "Archbishop" of Jerusalem, sends Peter to Cæsarea to stop the work carried on by Simon the Sorcerer (*Recogn.* I. 72, 73), and stands for seven days on the steps of the Temple proclaiming that Jesus is the Christ, while Saul, here also represented as from first to last the "enemy" of Peter and of James, is making havock of the Church. In the *Apostolic Constitutions*, a work probably of the third or fourth century, he appears with the Twelve (here also distinguished from the son of Alphæus), (Book VI. 14), and gives rubrical directions for the lighting of lamps, and the Evening Prayer that was to accompany it (Book VIII. 35—37), and for prayers for the departed (Book VIII. 41). In accordance with the hints there given, the Eastern Churches, of which Antioch was the centre, claimed him as having laid down the order and pattern of their worship, and the *Liturgy of James* comes before us as one of the great representatives of what was in the third, and possibly in the second, century, the Eucharistic Service of the ancient Church, and James is commemorated in it as the prince of

Bishops, Apostles, and Martyrs (Trollope's *Liturgy of St James*, p. 130). The "brother of the Lord" has become the Ἀδελφόθεος, "the brother of the very God." (*Ibid.* p. 25.)

Wild and fantastic as are these imaginings, they are yet not without interest as shewing how powerfully the personality of James had impressed itself on the minds of his contemporaries and followers. Legends gather round the memory of a great man, not of a small one. And the character which is visible through all of them is that of one who continued all his life a Hebrew of the Hebrews, zealous for the Law, and devout in its observance, winning by his personal holiness the admiration and reverence of all who knew him. It is refreshing, however, to pass from the region of fables, and to tread on the safer ground—safer, though here, too, we need the caution which should attend all exercise of the historical imagination—of the inferences that may legitimately be drawn from what the New Testament writers tell us of the man, from what he tells us of himself. We have, then, present before us one whose personal work is limited to Jerusalem, who undertakes no far-distant journeys. Such a life tends naturally to the devout, contemplative, ascetic pattern of religion. It keeps itself "unspotted from the world." Its practical activity is limited to "visiting the fatherless and widows in their affliction." The days pass by in a calm unbroken order, and the outer stirrings of the world scarcely ruffle it. And the life was spent in great part, at least, in company with the two Apostles, St Peter and St John. We can think of James as delighting in their converse, interchanging thoughts with them, learning from them, and in his turn teaching them, so that, as we have seen (p. 9), his words and phrases are often theirs, and theirs are his. And there also, for part of the time, must have been the Publican-Apostle, writing his Gospel for the Hebrews, yet writing it, there seems reason to believe, in Greek as well as Hebrew, for the twelve tribes that were scattered abroad, to whom St James addressed his Epistle. May we not think of the two as communing together as the work went on; the brother of the Lord imparting to the Evangelist the genealogy of the house of David, which was treasured among the records of his lineage, and the events, as he remembered or had heard them, of the Birth and Infancy of the Christ, and reading the Sermon on the Mount, in which he found the "royal law, the perfect law of freedom;" and of which accordingly we find so many echoes in the Epistle (p. 8)? From time to time there appears in Jerusalem one of wider thoughts and wider work, whom many of the Church at Jerusalem hated and suspected. James does not hate or suspect, and holds out the right hand of fellowship, but he feels that he has a vocation and ministry of his own, and his form of life and type of thought remain as they were, but little influenced by the teaching of the Apostle of the Gentiles. And Luke comes with St Paul, and the wide culture and sympathies of the beloved physician enable him to understand, better than others, the character of the Bishop of Jerusalem, outwardly so different from, essentially so in harmony with, the character of his friend, and he resolves that, as far as in him lies, the false rumours of an antagonism between them which had gone abroad and gained acceptance, shall be shewn to be not facts, but the reverse of facts, engendered by the father of lies. And the life thus calm and tranquil is naturally given to study as well as prayer and good works. The Holy Scriptures are naturally the chief object of those studies, but his early knowledge as a Galilæan, and his frequent intercourse with the Hellenistic pilgrims of the Dispersion, who came up to keep their Pentecost or other feasts at Jerusalem, made him familiar with the Greek version of those Scriptures, and so with the books which the Alexandrian Jews had added to the Hebrew volume. His Epistle shews how much he valued the practical teaching of one of those books, how he found in the Son of Sirach one who, like himself, had sought for wisdom and had not sought in vain. The parallelisms with that book are, as the following table will shew, nearly as numerous as those with the Sermon on the Mount.

James i. 5.	Ecclus. xx. 15, xli. 22.
...... i. 8.	.... i. 28, ii. 12.
...... i. 12.	.... i. 11, 16, 18.

INTRODUCTION.

James i. 12.	Ecclus. xv. 11.
...... i. 19.	.... v. 11, xx. 7.
...... i. 23.	.... xii. 11.
...... i. 25.	.... xiv. 23, xxi. 23.
...... iii. 5.	.... xxviii. 10.
...... iii. 6.	.... xxviii. 19 (?).

Yet another book, the work, probably, of a contemporary, written, as some have thought[1], by the Jew of Alexandria, eloquent and mighty in the Scriptures, to whom many critics, from Luther onwards, have assigned the authorship of the Epistle to the Hebrews, must have attracted him by its very title, the Wisdom of Solomon, and with this also we find not a few interesting and suggestive parallelisms.

James i. 11.	Wisd. ii. 8.
...... i. 12.	...... v. 7.
...... i. 17.	...... vii. 17—20.
...... i. 20.	...... xii. 10.
...... i. 23.	...... vii. 26.
...... ii. 21.	...... x. 5.
...... iv. 14.	...... iii. 16, v. 9—14.

We picture such a man to ourselves as grave and calm, for the most part silent, but when speaking, letting fall words that were as seeds that germinated and took root in the souls of others, indifferent to the luxuries and comforts of life, honouring the poor more than the rich, visiting the fatherless and the widow, accompanying the Elders of the Church when they anointed the sick with oil in the hope of their recovery, slow to judge, calming by his saintly meekness the angry passions of contending parties, adopting the policy of non-resistance in times of persecution. Not without cause did men speak of him as emphatically the "just, or righteous, one" as presenting a type of character after the pattern of His who was emphatically the Just One, Jesus Christ the Righteous (Matt. xxvii. 19; Luke xxiii. 47; Acts iii. 14, vii. 52; 1 John ii. 1). The frequent occurrence of that title either in its Greek or Latin form (as in

---

[1] See Two Papers on *The Writings of Apollos* in Vol. I. of the *Expositor*.

the *Justus* of Acts i. 23, xviii. 7; Col. iv. 11) seems to indicate that it was used somewhat freely of those who aimed at a higher righteousness than that of the Scribes and Pharisees.

So far as we may think of such a one as James the Just as needing refreshment after the strain of worship and of work, some subtle touches in the Epistle lead us to think of that refreshment as found by him, as by all pure and simple souls, in the forms of life around him. To consider the lilies of the field, to dwell lovingly on what he calls the comeliness, not of the fashion, but of the *face* of each fair flower (see Note on I. 10), to find a quiet joy, as St John is said to have done in his old age (see note on ch. iii. 7), in the power of man to tame the wildness, and even to win the affection, of bird or beast,—this also we may think of as entering into the life of the brother of the Lord, and teaching him new lessons in the wisdom which he sought. Christendom has presented many types of saintliness, more intense and vehement, more mystic and spiritual, with wider thoughts, or at least a freer utterance, of the mysteries of God. It was well that the Apostolic age should present one type such as this, in which holiness appeared mainly as identical with Wisdom; that this should be as much the special characteristic of St James, as Faith was of St Paul, and Hope of St Peter, and Love of the beloved disciple. That type has happily not been without its representatives in later ages of the Church. In Macarius of Egypt, in Thomas à Kempis, in our own Bishop Wilson, we trace the same ideal of life, the aim at that wisdom which cometh from above, and is first pure and then peaceable, gentle, and carrying with it the persuasive power of gentleness. The life of St James was well characterised by Eusebius (*Hist.* II. 23), as marked by "the highest philosophy." The Liturgy of the Greek Church as happily attaches the epithet "Wise" rather than Just, to the "brother of the Lord," and commemorates "the marvellous and ineffable mysteries" which were made known to him by the "Wisdom of the incarnate Lord" who vouchsafed to be his Teacher

CHAPTER II.

TO WHOM WAS THE EPISTLE ADDRESSED?

1. The letter which bears the name of James purports to be addressed to the "twelve tribes that are scattered abroad" (literally **in the dispersion**. See note on ch. i. 1). No other Epistle takes so wide a range. St Peter's, which comes nearest to it, does not extend beyond the section of the "dispersion" that was to be found in the northern and central provinces of Asia Minor. This contemplates nothing less than all the families of Israel, and, as far as they are concerned, is, in the fullest sense of the word, a Catholic or Universal Epistle.

On the other hand, there seems, at times, to be an implied limitation. He writes to those who "hold the faith of the Lord Jesus Christ" (ch. ii. 1), who have His worthy (or **noble**) Name called upon them (ch. ii. 7), who live in the expectation of His coming (ch. v. 7). Seen from one point of view, the Epistle seems a call to the outward Israel, such as the preaching of the Baptist had been, to be true to their calling, to live by the light they had, to conquer the besetting sins of their race. Seen from another, it is an earnest appeal to the Israelites who had accepted Jesus as the Christ, to be on their guard, lest those sins should reappear in the new society of the Church of God. From yet a third stand-point it seems to be addressed specially to the Churches of Judæa. It speaks of forms of persecution and oppression (ch. ii. 6, 7, v. 4), which obviously refer directly to the acts of violence that followed on the death of Stephen (Acts ix. 2), and were renewed under Herod Agrippa I. (Acts xii. 1, 2).

2. We shall perhaps be better able to understand the features which the Epistle thus presents to us, if we endeavour to realise the position of the writer. The Church of Jerusalem was committed to his special charge. All the notices of his life, historical, traditional, legendary, represent him as con-

fining himself to that special work, as never leaving the Holy City, as being a constant worshipper in the Temple. But every feast in every year brought to Jerusalem representatives of the "dispersion" from "every nation under heaven" (Acts ii. 5). Taking the list of those who were present on the day of Pentecost, we find among them those of Parthia and Media and Elam (Persia), who were descendants of the Ten Tribes that had been carried into exile by the river of Gozan and in the cities of the Medes by Shalmaneser (2 Kings xvii. 6); the dwellers of Mesopotamia, who were of the children of the Babylonian captivity (2 Kings xxiv. 14—16, xxv. 11); those of Egypt, who traced their settlement in Alexandria to the invasion of Ptolemy-Lagus (Joseph. *Ant.* XII. 1); others, as in the case of the eunuch of Acts viii. 27, who, in the reign of Manasseh, had been carried off by Psammetichus (as in the history of the Septuagint that bears the name of Aristeas), and were known, even in the time of the prophet Zephaniah, as the people "of the daughter of my dispersed beyond the rivers of Ethiopia" (Zeph. iii. 10). Lastly, there were those whom the war with Pompeius had scattered over every province of the Roman Empire and had planted in large numbers in Rome itself, those who had made their way from Alexandria to the parts of Libya about Cyrene, the more isolated settlements of Arabia and of Crete. With some of these, at least, St James would come into contact. In those who came from Egypt he might find thoughts in some measure in harmony with his own. The Therapeutæ (="healers of the soul," or, perhaps, "followers of the devout life"), who were leading a devout ascetic life on the shores of the Lake Mareotis in the Delta of the Nile, never tasting animal food nor wine, praising God in solemn chants and antiphonal hymns (Euseb. *Hist.* II. 17); the disciples of Philo, dwelling much on the attainment of a true philosophy as the highest aim of man, and identifying the Divine Word or Logos with the Giver of all wisdom and knowledge; those who brought with them the sapiential books which were studied among the Alexandrian Jews, the Wisdom of the Son of Sirach, and the more recent work known as the Wisdom of Solomon, probably by a contemporary, possibly, as some have inferred from numerous coincidences of thought and language, by the author of the Epistle to the Hebrews prior to his acceptance of the faith of Christ[1]. These he would welcome as manifesting in their various forms the search after the life of heavenly wisdom to which he himself was devoted. But in most of those who came he would note, with shame and sorrow, the same defects as those which he found among his own countrymen, the same greed of gain (ch. iv. 1, 2), the same respect of persons (ch. ii. 1—7), the same wrangling and bitterness in debate (ch. iii. 1—12). They relied upon their faith in the dogma of Monotheism as a substitute for holiness of life (ch. ii. 19). They abhorred idols, and yet robbed their temples (Rom. ii. 22). They pleased not God, and were contrary to all men (1 Thess. ii. 15). The name of God was blasphemed among the Gentiles through their lamentable and shameful inconsistencies (Rom. ii. 24). In view of these evils, we may believe, St James was led to write to the Twelve Tribes of the Dispersion, to call them at least to live up to the ideal of the faith of Israel. It lay in the nature of the case, however, that those with whom he came most into contact were those who held the faith which he held, that Jesus was the Christ, and that being so, He was none other than the Lord of Glory (ch. ii. 1). Only in such as these could he find those who would be the bearers of his letter to the several centres of the Dispersion. Only among these could he feel any assurance that his letter would, in the first instance, gain a hearing. In these he saw those who were to be, in the Divine purpose, a purpose which they might forward or frustrate, the first-fruits of humanity (ch. i. 18). And therefore he writes, not as a prophet or moralist only, but as "the servant of the Lord Jesus Christ" (ch. i. 1). He is above all anxious that they, in their life as individuals and as a community, should not hold the faith in the Lord Jesus as a mere barren dogma, but should shew the fruits of their higher knowledge in "the meekness of wisdom," in a nobler and purer life (ch. iii. 13). Because he is writing to the Twelve Tribes at large, he does not dwell with any

[1] See Note, p. 33.

fulness on the higher mysteries of the Kingdom, but is content to call on them to live by the light they have, in the conviction that in so doing they would be led to know of the doctrine whether it were of God (John vii. 17). Because he is writing to those who shared his faith and hope, he does not shrink from the confession of his belief in Jesus as the Christ, or from pressing on the minds of those who were to read his letter the solemn thought that He was the Judge, and that His coming was not far off (ch. v. 7). But one who lived as St James, in one spot, the horizon of whose view was consequently within comparatively narrow limits, was certain to be impressed mainly with what he himself heard and saw. He would dwell on the scenes which he witnessed, or knew of as practised in the Christian synagogues of Judæa (ch. ii. 1—3), to the persecutions of which it had been the scene, and in which the wealthy aristocracy of the Sadducean priest-party—always, as he himself experienced and as Josephus testifies (*Ant.* XIII. 10. § 6; XX. 9. § 1; *Wars*, II. 8. § 14), conspicuous for their judicial cruelties—had taken the most prominent part (ch. ii. 6). He would point to the indifference which the richer Jews shewed towards the sufferings of the poor of Jerusalem at the time of the famine, and contrast it with the liberality of the Gentile converts whom they despised as outside the pale of the covenant of Israel (ch. ii. 15—18).

Such, it is believed, is the conclusion to which the phænomena of the Epistle lead. It will be seen that it takes in whatever element of truth is to be found in the less complete theories which look on it as addressed only to Jews as such or only to Jewish Christians, or only to the Churches of Judæa. We need not wonder, if we remember even the outlines of the history of the Apostolic Church, that it should be comparatively slow in finding its way into general acceptance, that though in one sense Catholic in its aim, and in due time recognised by that title, it did not occupy, in the history of the Canon of the New Testament, a position like that of the Gospels or the Epistles of St Paul. Read in the first instance in the Churches of the Circumcision only, bearing the name of the Teacher whom the party of the Judaisers, developed afterwards into the sect of the Ebionites, claimed as theirs, and whom they put forward, as in the Pseudo-Clementine *Homilies* and *Recognitions*, as the antagonist of St Paul, it was inevitable that its course should be more or less retarded. We may, perhaps, trace some indirect reference to its teaching in the Epistle to the Romans (ch. ii. 24; Rom. iii. 28), yet more clearly in the Epistle to the Hebrews (ch. ii. 21, 25; Heb. xi. 17, 31), and in that of Clement to the Church of Corinth, as in his use of St James's word for "double-minded" (c. 11), his quotation of the question, "Whence come wars and fightings among you?" (c. 46), and of the maxim that love "covers a multitude of sins" (c. 49), in his reference to the sacrifice of Isaac (c. 31), in his citation of the same words from Prov. iii. 34, that are quoted by St James (c. 30), in the prominence which he gives to the history of Rahab (c. 12), in his naming Abraham the friend of God (c. 68). Irenæus (IV. 16) reproduces the passage about Abraham (ch. ii. 21), and there are many parallelisms between its teaching and that of the *Shepherd of Hermas*. Comp.

Mand. xii. 5 with James iv. 7
.... xii. 6 .... iv. 12.
.... ix. 1 .... i. 8.
Vis. iii. 9 .... v. 4.

In the time of Origen it was known and read. The Peschito Syriac version included it, and recognized the writer as an Apostle. Eusebius, as we have seen, classed it among the books that some looked on as spurious, nor was it included in the Canon of the Muratorian fragment, though that list takes in, as has been said above, such books as the *Wisdom of Solomon*, and the *Shepherd of Hermas*. Finally, however, with the other *Antilegomena*, it won its way, as already stated, to a general acceptance, was received into the Canon by the Council of Laodicea, A.D. 320, and the third Council of Carthage, A.D. 397, and is not now likely to be displaced, except by those who, led by dogmatic prejudices, think lightly, as Luther once did[1], of its merits, or by whom the whole idea of an authoritative Canon of inspired writings is more or less rejected.

[1] The famous "Epistle of straw" appeared in a German New Testament in A.D. 1522, and though not formally retracted, was never reproduced in any later edition.

CHAPTER III.

THE DATE OF THE EPISTLE.

1. I have assumed so far that the Epistle was written at a comparatively early date, probably prior to the earliest of St Paul's Epistles, or even to the Council at Jerusalem of Acts xv. It remains, however, to give a more distinct view of the facts that lead to that conclusion.

2. First, then, we note the absence of any reference to the controversy as to the necessity of circumcision, which that Council was summoned to decide. It is scarcely conceivable that one writing after such a controversy had arisen, would, in addressing himself to Jews and Jewish Christians throughout the world, have refrained from any reference to it. Writing before, it would be perfectly natural that he should assume that the position which had been assigned by the more liberal Rabbis to the Proselytes of the Gate would be conceded to those also who added faith in Jesus as the Christ to their acceptance of the creed of Israel, and had been baptized in His Name and had received the gift of the Spirit. The case of Cornelius (Acts x. 47) might well seem to have ruled the question once and for all in the sense in which St James afterwards ruled it. Here then we get probable limits for the date of the Epistle, in that conversion on the one hand, in the Council of Jerusalem on the other.

3. It may be noted that on this view the Epistle itself supplies a probable clue to the origin of the controversy, and explains the language in which St James and the Apostles and Elders repudiate the action of those who had originated it. "Forasmuch as we have heard that certain which went out from us have troubled you with words, subverting your souls, saying, Ye must be circumcised and keep the Law; *to whom we gave no such commandment*" (Acts xv. 24). It lies on the sur-

face that there was one passage in the Epistle, which, though written with no such purpose, might easily, interpreted as the Pharisees would interpret it, seem to give a countenance to the position which they maintained. St James had written, "Whosoever shall keep the whole law, and yet offend in one point, he is guilty of all" (ch. ii. 10). How easy it would be for the Judaisers to lay hold of such words, and ignoring the fact that he was speaking of the Law, new and yet eternal, the Law of the King, and yet the Law of freedom, to represent him as insisting on the observance of the whole Mosaic Code, as urging that the neglect of circumcision and new moons and sabbaths stood on the same footing as the violation of the great Laws of duty which were not of to-day or yesterday!

4. The reference to the persecutions to which the brethren were exposed in ch. ii. 6, is, it will be noted, in the present tense. It indicates a stage of suffering which has not yet receded into the past of history. The two persecutions to which the Churches of Judæa were exposed prior to the Council of Jerusalem were, (1) that in which Saul, the Pharisee, made himself the tool of the Sadducean priesthood, and in which deeds of violence were done precisely corresponding to St James's description (Acts ix. 2), and (2) that in which Herod Agrippa, seeking probably to gain the support of that priesthood as well as of the people, took a leading part (Acts xii. 1, 2). It is on the death of James the son of Zebedee in that persecution that the brother of the Lord, as we have seen, first comes into a new prominence, and it is not an improbable supposition that it was in face of the new responsibilities thus imposed upon him, that he wrote the Epistle that bears his name.

5. Another coincidence will help us, it is believed, to approximate yet more closely to the date as to which we are enquiring. If we believe, as is shewn in the notes on ch. ii. 15—18 to be probable, that the words which speak of the contrast between the works of one who feeds the hungry and clothes the naked, and the dead faith of one who rests in an orthodox belief, refer, more or less directly, to the generous help that had been given by the disciples at Antioch to the suffering

poor at Jerusalem, we find fresh grounds for the conclusion already arrived at; and accepting the dates commonly received for the chronology of the Acts, we have the years between A.D. 44, the date of the help so given, and A.D. 51, the year of the Council, as the limits within which we may place the composition of the Epistle. In all probability, *i.e.* it was written while Paul and Barnabas were absent from Antioch on their first missionary journey (Acts xiii.), and it was when they returned from their labours that they found their work thwarted and threatened by the false interpretation which had been put upon its teaching. The probable reference to the name of Christian in ch. ii. 7 is, it is obvious, in agreement with this conclusion. It may be mentioned that the view here taken agrees in the main with that maintained by Alford (*Commentary*), by Neander (*Pflanzung und Leitung*, II. p. 576), and most recent Commentators, and is accepted, as far as the date of the Epistle is concerned, by Mr Bassett (*Introduction to Commentary*). Bishop Wordsworth (*Introduction to St James*), following Lardner and De Wette and the school of Commentators who see in St James's teaching that which was intended to correct inferences drawn from St Paul's, places it naturally after the Epistles to the Galatians and Romans, circ. A.D. 61. It may be questioned, however, in addition to the positive arguments for the earlier date and against the presence of any such purpose in St James's thoughts, whether copies of those Epistles were likely to have found their way to Jerusalem during St James's life-time. Apostolical epistles were not likely to be transcribed by the hundred and circulated broadcast in that early age, and the burden of proof lies on those who assume that copies of what was written for Rome or Galatia would be at once despatched by a special courier to the Bishop of Jerusalem. The date of A.D. 61 or 62, shortly before the martyrdom of James in the latter year, must therefore be rejected, as supported by no adequate proof, and as being against the balance of the circumstantial evidence which has been here adduced.

6. As to the place of composition, there is not even the

INTRODUCTION. 43

shadow of a doubt. Even if there were not, as has been said above, an unbroken consent of all historical, traditional, and legendary notices as to the continued residence of the Bishop of Jerusalem in the city which was, in modern language, his see, the local colouring of the Epistle would indicate with sufficient clearness where the writer lived. He speaks, as the prophets of Israel had done, of the early and the latter rain (ch. v. 7); the hot blast of the *Kausôn* or Simoom of the desert (ch. i. 11), the brackish springs of the hills of Judah and Benjamin (ch. iii. 11), the figs, the olives, and the vines with which those hills were clothed (ch. iii. 12),—all these form part of the surroundings of the writer. Storms and tempests, such as might have been seen on the sea of Galilee or in visits to Cæsarea or Joppa, and the power of man to guide the great ships safely through them, have at some time or other been familiar to him (ch. iii. 4).

CHAPTER IV.

ANALYSIS OF THE EPISTLE.

The structure of the Epistle is, as every reader will feel, altogether informal and unsystematic, and an analysis can hardly aim at more than tracking the succession of topics and indicating, where possible, the latent sequence of thought.

CHAP. I. Writing to those of whom he thinks as exposed to trials and temptations, he opens with words of comfort as to the work they are meant to do (1—4). That they may accomplish that work men want the wisdom which learns the lessons of experience, and wisdom is given to those who ask for it in faith (5—7). In want of faith there is instability, and the secret reason why faith is in most men so weak is that they prefer the false riches to the true. Conquer that temptation, and trials lead straight on to the crown of life (8—12).

Nor must men think that they can plead destiny and God's Will as an excuse for yielding to temptation. That Will is absolutely righteous. Evil is found not in circumstances but in man's lust and appetite (13—17). From God comes all good and nothing but good, above all, the highest good of the Word of truth which regenerates our life (18—21). Well for us, if we receive that Word and do it ; woe for us, if we only think we have received it, and substitute a ritual observance for works of pitying love (22—27).

CHAP. II. How hollow such a ritual religion may be is seen even in the synagogues of believing Jews. They profess faith in Him who was poor Himself and the Friend of the poor, and in the very place where they meet to worship Him they insult the poor and act with base servility towards the rich. Small as men may think this fault, it is a wilful transgression of the law of Christ by which we are to be judged (1—13). It will profit such breakers of the Law little to say that they have maintained the faith of Israel in the Unity of the Godhead in the midst of the worshippers of Gods many and Lords many. Faith without works is dead, and the ultimate acquittal and acceptance of a man will depend not so much on what he has believed as on the manner in which belief has influenced practice (14—26).

CHAP. III. Nor was this the only evil of which the Christian synagogue was the scene. Men were struggling for preeminence as teachers, each with his doctrine and interpretation. Thence came wrangling and debate, and the tongue shot forth the fiery arrows of bitter words (1—8). To suppose that a man could be wise or religious while he was uttering curses and anathemas was as monstrous as any natural portent, salt and sweet water gushing from the same spring, figs borne by olive-trees, and the like (9—12). Far other than that was the true wisdom that comes from above. Let men look first on this picture and then on that, and so make their choice (13—18).

CHAP. IV. In strong contrast with the life regulated by such a wisdom is the unwisdom of those who think only of gratifying the promptings of their lower nature. From those promptings comes nothing but discords and confusion. Men must choose once more between the friendship of the world and that of God, between the lower and the higher life (1—8). Repentance, humility, the temper that refrains from judging, are the indispensable conditions of all true blessedness (9—12). The eagerness that throws its selfish aims and plans into the future, near or far, must be repressed by dwelling on the shortness and uncertainty of life (13—17).

CHAP. V. As if conscious that he had nearly reached the limit of his Epistle, the writer takes up the more solemn tone of the older prophets in his warnings to the rich. They little know the miseries which he foresees as close at hand, the swift judgment that is coming upon the oppressors and persecutors (1—7). What is a thought of terror for them is, however, one of encouragement and comfort for the patient sufferers. The "end of the Lord" for such, will be as full of blessing as that of Job and the prophets who had endured patiently in the days of old (7—11). A few more rules of life are needed for men's daily conduct. To abstain from rash and random oaths; to find in prayer and psalmody the true utterance of sorrow or of joy (12, 13); to trust to simple remedies and the prayer of faith in times of sickness (14, 15); to confess faults, one to another, in the belief that the prayer for forgiveness and other spiritual blessings is as mighty now as was Elijah's prayer for drought or rain (17, 18); to think not only or chiefly of saving ourselves, but to aim by prayer and counsel and act, at saving others (19, 20)—this is the true pattern of the life of Christ's disciples. Having said this, the writer has nothing more to say, and the Epistle ends.

ST. JAMES.

1—4. *Trials and their Purpose.*

JAMES, a servant of God and of the Lord Jesus Christ, 1
to the twelve tribes which are scattered abroad, greeting.

1—4. TRIALS AND THEIR PURPOSE.

1. *a servant of God and of the Lord Jesus Christ*] The description which the writer gives of himself throws no light on his identity. The term "servant," better **slave**, as one who had been bought with a price (1 Cor. vi. 20, vii. 23), was used of themselves by both St Peter (2 Pet. i. 1) and St Paul (Rom. i. 1; Titus i. 1). It might be claimed by either of the Apostles who bore the name of James, or by the brother of our Lord, or indeed by any believer. (1 Pet. ii. 16). It may be noted that this and ch. ii. 1 are the only passages in which St James names our Lord, and that the form in which the Name appears is identical with that in the Epistle from the Apostles and Elders assembled under St James's presidency, in Acts xv. 26.

to the twelve tribes which are scattered abroad] Literally, **that are in the dispersion.** The superscription is interesting as shewing that the ten tribes of the Kingdom of Israel, though they had been carried into a more distant exile than Judah and Benjamin, were thought of, not as lost and out of sight, but as still sharing the faith and hope of their fathers. So St Paul speaks of "the twelve-tribed nation" as "serving God day and night" (Acts xxvi. 7), and our Lord's promise that His twelve disciples should sit on thrones judging the twelve tribes of Israel (Matt. xix. 28), and the Apocalyptic vision of the sealing of the tribes (Rev. vii. 5—8) imply the same belief. The legend as to the disappearance of the Ten Tribes, which has given rise to so many insane dreams as to their identification with the Red Indians of America or our Anglo-Saxon forefathers, appears for the first time in the Apocryphal 2 Esdras (xiii. 39—47), a book probably of about the same date as the Revelation of St John.

The term, "the dispersion," the abstract noun being used for the concrete, had come to be a technical term for the Hellenistic and other Jews who were to be found within, or beyond, the limits of the Roman Empire. So the Jews ask whether our Lord will go "to the *dispersion* of (i. e. among) the Greeks" (John vii. 35). So St Peter writes to "the sojourners of the *dispersion*" in the provinces of Asia Minor

2 My brethren, count *it* all joy when ye fall into divers temp-
3 tations; knowing *this*, that the trying of your faith worketh

(1 Pet. i. 1). The term had probably come into use from the LXX. of Deut. xxviii. 25 ("There shall be a *dispersion* in all the kingdoms of the world"). So in Judith v. 19, Judah and Benjamin are said "to have come back from the *dispersion*," and the prayer of Nehemiah in 2 Macc. i. 27 is that "God would gather together his *dispersion*."

greeting] The salutation is the same as in the Epistle purporting to come from the Church over which St James presided, in Acts xv. 23. The literal meaning of the word is to rejoice, and the idiomatic use of the infinitive is a condensed expression of the full "I wish you joy." It was primarily a formula of Greek letter-writers, but it had been used by the LXX. for the Hebrew "peace" in Isaiah xlviii. 22, lvii. 21, and appears in the superscription of the letters of Antiochus in 2 Macc. ix. 19. It is the word used in the mock salutations of the soldiers in the history of the Passion, "*Hail*, King of the Jews" (Matt. xxvi. 49, xxvii. 29, xxviii. 9). In 2 John verses 10, 11 it is rendered by the colloquial English of "bidding God speed." It is not used in any other of the Epistles of the New Testament, St Paul and St Peter using the formula "grace and peace."

2. *count it all joy*...] We lose, in the English, the link which connects the wish for "joy" merged in our "greeting," with the thought which indicates how the wish may be realised even under conditions that seem most adverse to it. The transition may be noticed as characteristic of the style of the Epistle. Other examples of a like method will meet us as we go on. The Greek formula for "all joy" (literally, **every kind of joy**) suggests the thought of the varied elements of joy that were to be found in the manifold forms of trial.

into divers temptations] The word, as commonly in the New Testament, stands for trials that take the form of suffering, rather than for the enticements of pleasure. Comp. Luke xxii. 28; Acts xx. 19; 1 Cor. x. 13; 1 Pet. i. 6. Its use implies accordingly that those to whom the Epistle was written were passing through a time of adversity. This was true, more or less, of the whole Jewish race, everywhere, but it was specially true of those who being of the Twelve Tribes, also held the faith of the Lord Jesus Christ, and of those most of all who were most within the writer's view. Comp. 1 Thess. ii. 14; Heb. x. 32, 33, for the sufferings of Jewish and specially of Hebrew Christians. The word for "fall into" implies an unlooked-for concurrence of adverse circumstances.

3. *that the trying of your faith*] The word for "trying" implies at once a "test," and a "discipline" leading to improvement. The same phrase meets us, in conjunction also with "divers temptations," in 1 Pet. i. 7. Each was, perhaps, quoting what had become an axiom of the Church's life.

worketh patience] The Greek word always implies more than mere passive submission, the "*endurance* unto the end" of Matt. x. 22, xxiv. 13, the perseverance which does not falter under suffering.

patience. But let patience have *her* perfect work, that ye 4 may be perfect and entire, wanting nothing.

5—8. *Wisdom, and the Prayer that gains it.*

If any of you lack wisdom, let him ask of God, that giveth 5 to all *men* liberally, and upbraideth not; and it shall be

4. *But let patience have her perfect work*] Better, **and let endurance have a perfect work**, there being sequence of thought but not contrast. The word for "perfect" expresses the perfection of that which reaches its end, and so implies, possibly, a reference to our Lord's words in Matt. x. 22. The form of the counsel implies that the work might be hindered unless the will of those who were called to suffer co-operated with the Divine purpose. The sufferings must be borne joyfully as well as submissively.

that ye may be perfect and entire] The latter word implies completeness in all parts or regions of the spiritual life, as the former does the attainment of the end, the completeness of growth. The corresponding substantive is used for the "perfect soundness" of the restored cripple in Acts iii. 16; the adjective, in a like spiritual application, in 1 Thess. v. 23.

wanting nothing] The English is unfortunately ambiguous. Better, **failing** or **lacking in nothing**.

5—8. WISDOM, AND THE PRAYER THAT GAINS IT.

5. *If any of you lack wisdom*] As before, in verses 1 and 2, the prominent word of the preceding clause suggests the opening of the next, the word for "lack" being the same as the "wanting" in the previous verse. The prominence thus given to wisdom is characteristic of the teaching of St James (comp. ch. iii. 13—17). It is as though he had largely fashioned his thoughts of the spiritual life on the teaching of the Book of Proverbs and Ecclesiastes, perhaps also on the Wisdom of Solomon and Ecclesiasticus. Wisdom, in its good sense, stands, in New Testament language, as implying both a wider range of thought and a more direct influence on conduct than knowledge (1 Cor. xii. 8; Col. ii. 3).

that giveth to all men liberally] Literally, **simply**, but as to give simply, without reserve or *arrière pensée*, is to give freely, both the adverb and the corresponding noun often carried with them the idea of liberality (comp. Rom. xii. 8; 2 Cor. ix. 11, 13). The thought is that God gives *absolutely* all good gifts to those that ask Him (Matt. vi. 11), and the highest gift, that of the Spirit that imparts wisdom, is included in the promise (Luke xi. 13).

and upbraideth not] The word implies a contrast with human givers who too often, at the time or afterwards, mar their bounty with bitter and reproachful speeches. There seems here a direct allusion to the description in Ecclus. xx. 15, of "the gift of a fool," "He giveth little and upbraideth much," to the counsel "after thou hast given, upbraid not" (Ecclus. xli. 23). Not so, St James implies, does God give, though

6 given him. But let him ask in faith, nothing wavering: for he that wavereth is like a wave of the sea driven with the 7 wind and tossed. For let not that man think that he shall

we are more open to His reproaches than any who are the objects of our bounty can be to ours.

and it shall be given him] An obvious echo of our Lord's promise in Matt. vii. 7; Luke xi. 9.

6. *let him ask in faith*] The prominence thus given to faith at the very outset of the Epistle must be borne in mind in connection with the subsequent teaching of ch. ii. 14—26. Faith, i.e. trust in God, as distinct from belief in a dogma, is with him, as with St Paul, of the very essence of the spiritual life.

nothing wavering] Better, "nothing **doubting**." Another echo from our Lord's teaching (Matt. xxi. 21). The variations in the English version hinder us from seeing that St Paul, when he said that "Abraham *staggered* not at the promise of God...but was strong in faith" (Rom. iv. 20), was reproducing the very thought and language of St James. The primary idea of the verb used, as here, in the middle voice, is that of the inner "debating" which implies doubt. It does not involve the absolute negation of unbelief, though, as in Rom. iv. 20, it tends to this, but represents the state of one who meets the question, "Will God keep His promise?" now with *Yes*, and now with *No*. The words of our own poet,

"Faith and Unfaith can ne'er be equal powers,
Unfaith in aught is want of faith in all."
Tennyson's *Merlin and Vivien*.

reproduce the substance of St James's teaching.

he that wavereth is like a wave] Better, **he that doubteth**. The English play upon the word, though happy in itself, has nothing corresponding to it in the Greek. Wycliffe gives "doubt." Tyndal introduced "waver" in the previous clause, but kept "doubteth" in this.

driven with the wind and tossed] Better, **driven by the winds and blasts**, both words describing the action of a storm at sea, the latter pointing especially to sudden gusts and squalls. The image, true at all times and for all nations, was specially forcible for a people to whom, like the Jews, the perils of the sea were comparatively unfamiliar. Comp. the description of the storm in Prov. xxiii. 34 and the comparison of the wicked to the "troubled sea" in Isaiah lvii. 20. Popular speech likens a man who has no stedfastness to a ship drifting on the troubled waves of life. St James goes one step farther and likens him to the unresting wave itself. Now he is in the depths, now uplifted high. In Eph. iv. 14 the same image describes those who are "carried about by every wind of doctrine." So far as St James wrote from personal experience we trace, perhaps, a recollection of stormy nights upon the Sea of Galilee. If we could identify him with the son of Zebedee, we might think of him as remembering such a night as that of Matt. viii. 24 or John vi. 18.

7. *let not that man think*...] Faith, undoubting faith, is then the

receive any *thing* of the Lord. A double minded man *is* 8
unstable in all his ways.

9—11. *Riches, and their perishableness.*

Let the brother of low degree rejoice in that he is ex- 9
condition of the prayer for wisdom, as of all other prayers, being heard
and answered. Without it, the *No* excludes the *Yes*, which yet the
man will not quite abandon.

of the Lord] It is a question whether the Divine Title is used in the
Old Testament sense, for the Father, or, as generally, though not
exclusively, in the New Testament, for the Son. On the whole, looking (1) to the meaning of the word in ch. v. 7, 14, 15, (2) and to the
frequent use of "*God*" and "*the Father*," where Christ is not meant,
there seems a balance of evidence in favour of the latter meaning.
Christ also, not less than the Father, is thought of as giving or not
giving, in answer to prayer. Possibly, however, the word was used
without the thought of a distinction between the Divine Persons.

8. *A double minded man*...] The context shews that the man so described (the Greek word is not found in any earlier writer and may have
been coined by St James) is not the fraudulent man but the waverer,
trying to serve two masters (Matt. vi. 24), halting between two opinions
(1 Kings xviii. 21). It answers to the "*double heart*" (Heb. "*a heart
and a heart*") of Ps. xii. 2. In Ecclus. i. 28 we find the same thought,
though not the same word, "Come not unto the Lord *with a double
heart*," and again in Ecclus. ii. 12, where a woe is uttered against the
"sinner *that goeth two ways*," in company with "the fearful and fainthearted." Clement of Rome (i. 11) reproduces St James's word. The
construction of the sentence is doubtful, and may be taken either as
in the English text, or, with "he that doubteth" as the subject and
"double-minded, unstable" as predicates.

unstable] The Greek word is found in the LXX. of Isaiah liv. 11, where
the English version has "tossed with tempest." It is not found elsewhere in the New Testament, except as a various reading in ch. iii. 8,
but the corresponding noun is often used both literally and figuratively
(Luke xxi. 9; 1 Cor. xiv. 33; 2 Cor. vi. 5, xii. 20; James iii. 16 and the
LXX. of Prov. xxvi. 28). There is a slight change of imagery, and
the picture brought before us is that of a man who does not walk
straight onward, but in "all his ways" goes to and fro, now on this side,
now on that, staggering like a drunken man.

9—11. RICHES, AND THEIR PERISHABLENESS.

9. *Let the brother of low degree*] The Greek joins the sentence on to
the preceding with the conjunction which may be either "and," or "but,"
implying that there is a sequence of ideas of some kind. The train of
thought would seem to lie in the fact, as shewn in our Lord's words
(Matt. vi. 24) that the love of mammon is the most common source of
the "double-mindedness" which St James condemns, both in the poor and
in the rich. The "brother" is used, as commonly in the New Testa-

10 alted: but the rich, in that he is made low: because as the
11 flower of the grass he shall pass away. For the sun is no
sooner risen with a burning heat, but it withereth the

ment as meaning one of the brotherhood of Christ. The word Christian had probably not as yet come into use in the Churches of Judæa, and was, at any rate, used of the disciples by others rather than by themselves. "Of low degree" is, perhaps, somewhat too narrow a rendering. Better, **he that is lowly** or more simply "he that is low." The contrast with the rich man shews that "poverty" is the chief feature in the low estate spoken of.

rejoice] Better as elsewhere, **glory**, or **exult**.

in that he is exalted] Better, **in his exaltation**. His lowliness instead of being a thing to be ashamed of, was his true title to honour. Christ had marked him out as an heir of the Kingdom (Luke vi. 20; see ch. ii. 5). Man's estimate of honour and dishonour is reversed by God.

10. *But the rich, in that he is made low*] Better, **in his humiliation** or **lowliness**. The context implies that the rich man also is a "brother." Such an one was tempted to exult in his wealth as that which raised him above his fellow-men. The view which Christ had taught him to take was, that it placed him on a level lower than that of the poor. His true ground for exultation would be to accept that lower position, to glory in it, as it were, as St Paul gloried in his infirmities (2 Cor. xii. 9), and to make himself, by the right use of his wealth, a servant of servants unto his brethren. The two other interpretations which have been given of the words, (1) that suggested by the English, that the rich man is to rejoice when he is brought low by adversity, and (2) that the sentence is to be filled up not by an imperative but an indicative, "but the rich man" (on this assumption, not a "brother") "exults in what is indeed his degradation," are, it is believed, less satisfying. Possibly, still keeping the imperative, the words may be taken as ironical "let him glory in his shame." The whole passage, however interpreted, shews, like chap. iv. 11; 1 Pet. v. 6, the impression that had been made on the minds of the disciples by the teaching of their Master in Matt. xxiii. 12; Luke xiv. 11, xviii. 14.

because as the flower of the grass he shall pass away] This, so the train of thought runs, is that which is most humbling to the man of wealth. His riches are transient. They vanish often during life. He can carry nothing with him when he dies. For the third time in this chapter we notice a close parallelism of thought and language with St Peter (1 Pet. i. 24), both drawing from Isai. xl. 6, as a common source.

11. *For the sun is no sooner risen...but it withereth*] Better, **for the sun arose and withered**. The Greek has nothing that answers to "no sooner," and the verbs are throughout in the past tense as in a narrative. It is as though St James were using the form not of a similitude, but of a parable, apparently not without a reminiscence of some features of the Parable of the Sower (Matt. xiii. 6) and of the Sermon on the Mount (Matt. vi. 30).

with a burning heat] Better, **with the scorching heat**, probably the *Simoom*, or hot wind that blows from the desert in the early morning, as grass, and the flower thereof falleth, and the grace of the fashion of it perisheth: so also shall the rich *man* fade away in his ways.

12—15. *Temptation, and its history.*

Blessed *is* the man that endureth temptation: for when 12 he is tried, he shall receive the crown of life, which the

in Luke xii. 55. The whole description comes, as above, from Isaiah xl. 6. Comp. also Jonah iv. 8.

falleth...perisheth] Better, as continuing the narrative, **fell—perished**.

fade away] Better, perhaps, as expressing the force of the Greek passive, **be blighted**. The Greek verb is not found elsewhere in the New Testament, but meets us in the Wisd. of Sol. ii. 8, in a passage which may well have been present to the mind of the writer. An adjective derived from it is found in the "crown that fadeth not away," literally, **the amaranthine crown**, of 1 Pet. v. 4. See also 1 Pet. i. 4. The idea of the "fading" of earthly riches, the "unfading" character of heavenly, was another thought common to the two writers.

the grace of the fashion of it] Better, **the goodliness of its form**, literally, **of its face**. The first substantive is not found elsewhere in the New Testament.

in his ways] Literally, **in his goings** or **journeyings**, as in Luke xiii. 22, perhaps with a special reference to the restlessness in trading which shewed itself in the money-making Jews of Palestine. "Going" and "getting" (*poreuomai* and *emporeuomai*) made up the sum total of their ideal of life. Comp. chap. iv. 13. A various reading gives "in his *gettings*" here, as a possible meaning, but the balance of evidence is in favour of "goings."

12—15. TEMPTATION, AND ITS HISTORY.

12. *Blessed is the man that endureth temptation*] The mode of teaching by Beatitudes reminds us at once of the Sermon on the Mount, with which, it will be seen afterwards, the Epistle has so many points of contact. Stress is laid on "enduring" as distinct from simply "suffering," and the "temptation" is prominently, as in verse 2, that of suffering coming from without.

for when he is tried] Better, **when he has stood the trial**, the Greek adjective being applied, as in Rom. xiv. 18, xvi. 10, to one who has been tested and approved.

the crown of life] The image of the "crown" or **wreath** of the conqueror for the reward of the righteous is common both to St Peter who speaks of "the crown of glory" (1 Pet. v. 4) and to St Paul who speaks of "the crown of righteousness" (2 Tim. iv. 8). The "crown of life,"—i. e. of eternal life, which *is* the crown, is, however, peculiar to St James. The figurative use of the word is characteristic of the Son of Sirach (Ecclus. i. 11, 16, 18, xxv. 6), and of the LXX. of Proverbs (i. 9, iv. 9). In Wisd. v. 16, we have, in the Greek, the kindred word "diadem."

13 Lord hath promised to them that love him. Let no *man* say when he is tempted, I am tempted of God: for God cannot be tempted with evil, neither tempteth he any *man:* 14 but every man is tempted, when he is drawn away of his

which the Lord hath promised to them that love him] Here again it is a question whether "the Lord" is to be taken in its special New Testament sense, or generally of God. As before (see Note on verse 7) the balance turns in favour of the former, and the tense of the verb ("which the Lord promised"), as if referring to some special utterance, may lead us to think of such words as those of John xiv. 21, 23. A more general promise of the same kind to those that love the Lord is found in Ecclus. xxxiv. 16.

13. *Let no man say when he is tempted*] The thought of trial as coming from outward circumstances, and forming part of man's spiritual education, leads to a deeper inquiry as to its nature, and so passes on to the wider notion of temptation, which includes the allurements of desire as well as the trials of adversity. In both cases men found refuge from the reproof of conscience in a kind of fatalism. God had placed them in such and such circumstances; therefore, He was the author of the sin to which those circumstances had led. The excuse is one which presents itself to men's minds at all times, but here also there is a special point of contact with the Son of Sirach: "Say not thou, it is through the Lord that I fell away" (Ecclus. xv. 11). It may be noted that the popular Pharisaism, which taught a doctrine of necessity (Joseph. *Ant*. XVIII. 1. § 3; *Wars*, II. 8. § 14) while speculatively maintaining also the freedom of man's will, was likely to develope into this kind of practical fatalism.

I am tempted of God] The order of the Greek words is more emphatic, **It is from God that I am tempted.** ἀπὸ θεοῦ πειράζομαι

for God cannot be tempted with evil] The English "cannot be tempted" answers to a Greek verbal adjective, not used elsewhere in the New Testament or in the LXX. version of the Old, and not found in Classical Greek. Its meaning as used in later Greek writers, is simply "untried," and so "unversed in," and it has been maintained that it is so used here, but the context makes it almost certain that St James used it in the sense of "*untempted*." At first it might seem as if this assertion did not meet the thought to which it appears to be answer, but the latent premiss of the reasoning seems to be that no one tempts to evil, who has not been first himself tempted by it. If men shrank from the blasphemy of affirming that of God, they ought to shrink also from the thought that He could ever tempt them to evil. He who was absolutely righteous, could not be the originator of sin. He *tries* men, but does not *tempt* them.

neither tempteth he any man] Better, **and He** (the pronoun is emphatic) **tempteth no one.**

14. *when he is drawn away of his own lust, and enticed*] Both the participles are primarily used of the way in which animals are taken, the first of capture by the hook or noose, as with fish or the crocodile (Herod. II. 70), the second of beasts or birds which are attracted by food

own lust, and enticed. Then when lust hath conceived, it 15
bringeth forth sin: and sin, when it is finished, bringeth
forth death.

16—18. *God and His perfect gifts.*

Do not err, my beloved brethren. Every good gift and 16
17

set for them as a bait. Both words had come to be used figuratively of sensual passion, the latter twice by St Peter (2 Pet. ii. 14, 18), and the imagery that follows here suggests the thought that St James had the picture of the harlot of Prov. vii. 6—23 present to his thoughts. There the "young man void of understanding" yields to her allurements as "a bird hasteth to the snare." "Lust," or rather, **desire**, in its widest sense, including desire for safety, riches, ease, as well as sensual pleasure, is to man's will as the harlot-temptress of that picture. The temptations of which the earlier verses of the Chapter had spoken are thus, though no longer prominent, not excluded. Adversity and persecution expose men to the evil solicitations of their lower nature, to love of ease and safety, no less than luxury and prosperity. In both "desire" tempts the will to depart from what it knows to be the will of God.

15. *when lust hath conceived, it bringeth forth sin*] The image suggested in the previous verse is developed with an almost startling boldness. The will that yields to desire in so doing engenders evil. And as from that fatal embrace, there comes first the conception and then the birth of sin. But sin also grows; it has its infancy of purpose and its maturity of act; and so the parable is continued. Sin, in its turn, grows up, and by its union with the will becomes the mother of a yet more terrible offspring, and that offspring is Death, the loss of the true life of the soul, which consists in its capacity for knowing God. The second of the two words rendered "bringeth forth" (better, perhaps, **engendereth**) differs from the first, and seems, as a less common word, to have been used for extraordinary or monstrous births (such e.g. as a woman's bearing four or five children), and so is appropriate here. The word occurs again in verse 18, where see note. In looking at the allegory as a whole we note: (1) its agreement as to the relation of sin and death, with the teaching of St Paul (Rom. v. 12); (2) its resemblance to like allegories in the literature of other nations, as in the well-known Choice of Hercules that bears the name of Prodicus, in which Pleasure appears with the garb and allurements of a harlot; (3) its expansion in the marvellous allegory of Sin and Death in Milton's *Paradise Lost* (B. II. 745—814), where Satan represents Intellect and Will opposed to God, Sin its offspring, self-generated, and Death the fruit of the union of Mind and Will with Sin. In the incestuous union of Sin and Death that follows and in its horrid progeny, Milton seems to have sought to shadow forth the shame and foulness and misery in which even the fairest forms of sin finally issue.

16—18. GOD AND HIS PERFECT GIFTS.

16. *Do not err...*] The absolute goodness of God had been presented so far on its negative side as excluding all origination of every perfect gift is from above, and cometh down from the Father of lights, with whom is no variableness, neither evil. But the writer feels that that is but a partial view. It has a brighter aspect, more full of hope and blessing, and the error against which he protests is chiefly hurtful as excluding that aspect from its due influence on faith and conduct.

17. *Every good gift and every perfect gift*] The two nouns are different in the Greek, the first expressing the abstract *act of giving*, the second the *gift* as actually bestowed. The perfection of the one flows from the goodness of the other. The "perfect gift" carries our thoughts beyond all temporal blessings which, though good, have yet an element of incompleteness, to the greater gifts of righteousness and peace and joy; the gift, i.e. of the Holy Spirit, which is the crowning gift of all. Singularly enough, the axiom, if we may so call it, falls into the cadence of a Greek hexameter, and it is conceivable that it may have been a quotation from a poem, or possibly from an early Christian hymn. Like instances of metre are found, besides the direct quotations in 1 Cor. xv. 33, Tit. i. 12, in the Greek of Heb. xii. 13 and Rev. xix. 12. The whole passage reminds us once more of the Sermon on the Mount (Matt. vii. 11) and of the parallel promise in Luke xi. 13.

is from above] The perfect gifts come then, as the new birth of the soul comes, from Heaven, not from Earth (comp. John iii. 3, as in the margin), as does the true wisdom (chap. iii. 15, 17). The prominence of the word and the thought in the Epistle is one of the links that connect it with the Gospel of St John, in which a like prominence is traceable (John iii. 7, 31, xix. 11).

from the Father of lights] The plural is used to express the thought, that light in all its forms, natural (as in the "great lights" of Ps. cxxxv. 7), intellectual, spiritual, is an efflux from Him "who is light, and in whom is no darkness at all" (1 John i. 5). This axiom as to the Divine Nature was also common to the two great teachers of the Church of the Circumcision, as it was to the teaching of the Apostle of the Gentiles, when he describes the children of God as being also "children of light" (Eph. v. 8). There may possibly be a reference to the Urim and Thummim, the "lights" and "perfections" which symbolised God's gifts of wisdom in its highest forms (Exod. xxviii. 30; Lev. viii. 8; Deut. xxxiii. 8). Comp. also Ps. xlviii. 3.

with whom is no variableness] The noun is primarily a scientific term (our English *parallax* presents a cognate word) as expressing the change of position, real or apparent, of the stars. Here it is apparently suggested by the word "lights," which primarily conveyed the thought of the heavenly bodies as the light-givers of the world. They, St James seems to say, have their changes, but not so their Creator and their Father.

shadow of turning] i.e. **shadow caused by turning**. The latter word, from which we get our "*trope*," and "*tropic*," is applied, as in the LXX. of Job xxxviii. 33; Deut. xxxiii. 14, to the apparent motion of the lights of heaven, and so to any changes. The former is also a quasi-scientific term, applied to the effect produced on the sun's disc shadow of turning. Of his own will begat he us with the 18 word of truth, that we should be a kind of firstfruits of his creatures.

by the moon in an eclipse. St James does not appear to use the terms with any very strict accuracy, but the fact that he employs them at all, and that they occur nowhere else in the New Testament, is in itself interesting as connecting him with the form of wisdom described in Wisd. vii. 17—20, which deals with "the alterations of the turning of the sun" (the two terms are nearly identical with those which St James uses) and "the change of seasons." Science, he seems to say, deals with the mutability of phænomena. Faith, and therefore Wisdom, rest on the immutability of God.

18. *Of his own will begat he us*] The construction of the Greek is participial, **willing he begat us**, and is parallel to that of Col. ii. 18, which, rightly rendered, runs "let no man willing, i.e. by the exercise of his will, deprive you...." The word implies the rejection of the thought either of a destiny constraining the Divine Will, or of chance and, as it were, random impulses, and the reference of our higher spiritual birth to His deliberate Will. Here again we have a parallelism with St John "born....not of the will of man, but of God" (John i. 13), and with St Peter (1 Pet. i. 23).

The word for "begat" is the same as the second "bringeth forth" in verse 15, and is obviously used here, with the general sense of "engendering" or "begetting," to emphasise the contrast between the process which ends in death and that which issues in a higher life. Here also, though the birth was not monstrous, it was out of the common course of Nature, and therefore the unusual word was rightly employed again.

with the word of truth] So our Lord makes Truth, the "word which is truth," the instrument of the consecration or sanctification of His people (John xvii. 17—19). The "word of truth" cannot have here the higher personal sense which the WORD or **Logos** has in John i. 1, but it is something more than the written Word of the Old Testament Scriptures, or even the spoken word of preachers. It is the whole message from God to man, of which the written or spoken word is but one of the channels, and which to those who receive it rightly is the beginning of a higher life. Comp. Matt. xiii. 19; Mark iv. 14.

a kind of firstfruits of his creatures]. The meaning of the term is traced back to the Jewish ritual of Lev. xxiii. 10; Deut. xxvi. 2. The sheaf of the firstfruits was offered as part of the Passover celebration. On their entry into Canaan the Israelites were to offer the firstfruits of the land (Deut. xxvi. 2). In each case the consecration of the part was a symbol and earnest of that of the whole. So St James speaks of the "brethren" who have been born to a higher life, not only as better than others, but as the pledge of a fuller harvest. So St Paul speaks of Christ being "the firstfruits of them that sleep" (1 Cor. xv. 20), of a convert being "the firstfruits of Achaia" (1 Cor. xvi. 15). St John agrees, as usual, more closely with St James, and describes "the redeemed from the earth" of Rev. xiv. 4 as "the firstfruits unto God

19—21. *Man's wrath, and God's righteousness.*

19 Wherefore, my beloved brethren, let every man be swift
20 to hear, slow to speak, slow to wrath: for the wrath of man
21 worketh not the righteousness of God. Wherefore lay apart
all filthiness and superfluity of naughtiness, and receive

and to the Lamb." Christians are called and made what they are by the grace of God, that they may shew of what elevation humanity is capable. Comp. Rom. xi. 16.

19—21. MAN'S WRATH, AND GOD'S RIGHTEOUSNESS.

19. *Wherefore*] The better MSS. give "Ye know this...but let every man."

my beloved brethren] The formula of address was common to all the four great writers of the Apostolic Church. We find it in St Paul (1 Cor. xv. 58), in St Peter (2 Pet. iii. 14, 15), in St John (1 John ii. 7, iii. 2). In the last two instances, however, the word "brethren" is wanting.

let every man be swift to hear] From the general thought of the high ideal of life implied in the new birth from God, St James passes to the special aspect of that ideal which was most in contrast with the besetting sin of his countrymen. To him speech was of silver, and silence of gold. In this as in many other passages of his Epistle, he echoed the teaching of the sapiential books of the Old Testament (Prov. xiii. 3, xiv. 29, xvii. 27; Eccles. v. 2) yet more, perhaps, of those of the Apocrypha. So we find "Be swift to hear" in Ecclus. v. 11, and maxims of a like nature in Ecclus. xx. 7. The "slow to wrath" follows on "slow to speak" as pointing to the crucial test of character. If it were hard at all times to be "slow to speak," it was harder than ever when men were roused to anger.

20. *the wrath of man...*] Better, **A man's wrath**, so as to represent the absence of the article in the original. By "the righteousness of God" —the phrase is common to St James and St Paul (Rom. x. 3; 2 Cor. v. 21; Phil. iii. 9)—is meant the righteousness which God requires and which He also gives. The besetting sin of the Jews was to identify their own anger against what seemed sin and heresy with the Will of God, to think that they did God service by deeds of violence (John xvi. 2), that they were thus working out His righteousness. The teaching is again after the pattern of the purely ethical books of the Old Testament (Eccles. vii. 9). The MSS. give two forms of the verb rendered "work;" the commonly received one, which conveys the thought, "does not work out or bring to completeness," and that of the better MSS. which means simply, "does not work, or practise."

21. *lay apart all filthiness...*] The cognate adjective is found in its literal sense in ch. ii. 2, and figuratively in Rev. xxii. 11. A kindred noun appears in a like combination in "the putting away of the *filth* of the flesh" of 1 Pet. iii. 21 and in the LXX. of Prov. xxx. 12. The word with meekness the engrafted word, which is able to save your souls.

22—25. *Doers and Hearers.*

But be ye doers of the word, and not hearers only, deceiving your own selves. For if any be a hearer of the

22

23

points not specifically to what we call "sins of impurity," but to every form of sin, including the "wrath" of the preceding verse, as defiling the soul.

superfluity of naughtiness] Better, **excess of malice**, i. e. excess characterised by malice. The English "naughtiness," though used in the 16th century, as by Latimer and Shakespeare, as equivalent to "sin" or "wickedness," has gradually lost its sharpness, and has come to be applied almost exclusively to the faults of children. The Greek word, though, like the Latin word from which *malice* comes, originally generic in its meaning, had come to be associated mainly (as in Eph. iv. 31; Col. iii. 8; 1 Pet. ii. 1) with the sins that have their root in wrath and anger, rather than with those that originate in love of pleasure, and so carries on the sequence of thought.

receive with meekness the engrafted word] The order of the words in the original is more emphatic, **but in meekness** (as contrasted with wrath and malice) **receive ye**. The "engrafted word" is that which was before referred to as the instrument by which the new and better life was engendered. The English "engrafted" suggests one process of growth somewhat too definitely, and **implanted** would be a better rendering. The word is not found elsewhere in the New Testament (the Greek word in Rom. xi. 17 is more specific), but, like so many of St James's phrases, appears in the sapiential books of the Apocrypha (Wisd. xii. 10, "their malice was *bred* in them"). We note the agreement of his teaching with that of the Parable of the Sower, where the Seed is the "Word," and the conditions of its fertility are found in "the honest and good heart" (Matt. xiii. 23), free from prejudice and bitterness. Moral discipline, the putting away of that which defiles, is the right preparation for the highest spiritual life.

which is able to save your souls] The words express at once the power, and the limits of the power. There was in the implanted word, taken in its widest sense, the promise and the potency of salvation, yet it did not work as by compulsion or by a charm, but required the co-operation of man's will. So, later on, St James speaks of God Himself as being "*able* to save" (chap. iv. 12).

22—25. DOERS AND HEARERS.

22. *But be ye doers of the word, and not hearers only*] The thought is the same, though illustrated by a different similitude, as that of the closing verses of the Sermon on the Mount (Matt. vii. 24—28). The reference to the "hearers of the word" confirms the explanation given above of the Word of the Truth. It is not primarily the *written* word,

word, and not a doer, he is like unto a man beholding his
24 natural face in a glass: for he beholdeth himself, and goeth

for then we should have the "reader," not the "hearer," nor Christ as the Incarnate WORD, but the spoken message from God to the soul of man—*"Be ye doers;"* literally, **"become,"** as though life were a continued process of such "becoming," the condition not being that in which men find themselves by nature.

deceiving your own selves] The word is etymologically more definite than that commonly used for deceiving, and implies strictly the self-deception, if one may so speak, of bad logic. The hypocrite knew the major premiss; "The doers, not the hearers, are blessed," but though conscience supplied the minor, "I am a hearer, not a doer," he shut his eyes to it and failed to draw the conclusion. The use of the word in the LXX., as e.g. in Gen. xxxi. 7, 41; Exod. viii. 29, shews, however, that it had come to be used in the general sense of "cheating" or "defrauding," and it may be questioned, therefore, how far the special sense is to be pressed here.

23. *he is like unto a man...*] The instance is chosen to illustrate the nature of the *paralogism* or fallacy by which the man deceived himself. It lies, as said above, in forgetting the self-knowledge which should form a premiss in his argument, and reasoning as if it did not exist.

beholding his natural face] Literally, **the face of his birth**, that which he was born with. The latter word might seem at first almost superfluous, but it serves to point the spiritual interpretation. That which the man sees in the mirror of the Divine Word, is the revelation of himself, as he is by nature (comp. 1 Cor. xiv. 24, 25), weak, sinful, "double-minded." That revelation is meant to lead him to seek for supernatural strength to rise to the higher life. The word for "beholding" implies more than a passing glance, the man *contemplates* the reflection of his face (see Matt. vii. 3; Luke xii. 24).

in a glass] Better, **in a mirror**. The word is the same as in 1 Cor. xiii. 12. The mirrors in use among the Jews, Greeks, and Romans were of polished metal, and as these presented a less perfect image than our modern mirrors, to see through, i.e. by means of, a mirror had become among the later Rabbis, as well as with St Paul, a proverbial phrase for man's imperfect knowledge of divine things. Here, however, stress is laid on the fact that the mirror does supply, in some measure, the self-knowledge which the man could not attain without it. The sapiential books of the Apocrypha present two interesting illustrations drawn from the same source (Wisd. vii. 26; Ecclus. xii. 11). It is possible, though it can hardly be insisted on, that there is an emphasis on a *man's* casual way of looking at a mirror, and the more careful gaze supposed to be characteristic of a *woman*.

24. *For he beholdeth himself...*] The Greek gives a subtle variation in the tenses. "For he **beheld** himself" (the momentary act), and **hath gone away** (the completed departure continuing in the present), and **forgat** (the oblivion coming and being completed in a moment). The

his way, and straightway forgetteth what manner of *man* he was. But whoso looketh into the perfect law of liberty, and 25 continueth *therein*, he being not a forgetful hearer, but a doer of the work, this *man* shall be blessed in his deed.

26, 27. *True and false Religion.*

If any *man* among you seem to be religious, and bridleth 26

mode of stating a similitude in the form of a narrative related as belonging to the past is characteristic of St James's style. See note on verse 11.

25. *But whoso looketh...*] The word involves primarily the idea of stooping down and bending over that on which we look, as with a fixed gaze. See for its literal use Mark xvi. 5; Luke xxiv. 12, and for its spiritual application, "which things the angels desire *to look into*," in 1 Pet. i. 12. In Ecclus. xiv. 23, it is used of the "prying in," the eager gaze of the seeker after wisdom; in xxi. 23 of the intrusive gaze of the fool. Here it implies, like our word "attend," the fixing the whole mind on that which the mirror of the Divine Word discloses to us, but as the act itself might, like the "beholding" of the previous verse, be but transient, St James adds the further condition, "and continueth therein."

the perfect law of liberty] The words appear at first to be wide and general, and to echo the language in which Psalmists and others had spoken of "the law of the Eternal" (Pss. xix. 7, cxi. 7, cxix. 1). On the other hand, we have to remember that at the Council at which St James presided, the law of Moses, as such, was described as "a yoke" of bondage (Acts xv. 10), even as St Paul spoke of it (Gal. v. 1), and that our Lord had spoken of the Truth as that by which alone men could be made "free indeed" (John viii. 32). It follows from this, almost necessarily, that St James speaks of the new Law, the spiritual code of ethics, which had been proclaimed by Christ, and of which the Sermon on the Mount remains as the great pattern and example. That Law was characterised as giving to the soul freedom from the vices that enslave it. To look into that Law and to continue in it was to share the beatitudes with which it opened. That the writer was familiar with that Sermon we shall see at well nigh every turn of the Epistle.

being not a forgetful hearer, but a doer of the work] Literally, **becoming not a hearer of forgetfulness.** The construction is the same as in the "steward of injustice" for the "unjust steward" (Luke xvi. 8, xviii. 6), the genitive of the characteristic attribute being used instead of the adjective. As the one clause balances the other the words that follow probably meant **an active worker** or "doer." In any case the article, as in the Greek, should be omitted. "**a doer of work.**"

this man shall be blessed in his deed] Once again, as if shewing on what his thoughts had been dwelling, as the law of liberty, St James returns to the formula of a beatitude, and brings together, in so doing, the beginning and the end of the Sermon on the Mount.

not his tongue, but deceiveth his own heart, this *man's*
27 religion *is* vain. Pure religion and undefiled before God
and the Father is this, To visit the fatherless and widows
in their affliction, *and* to keep himself unspotted from the
world.

26, 27. TRUE AND FALSE RELIGION.

26. *If any man among you seem to be religious*] Better, **If any man thinks that he is religious**. The Greek adjective is one which expresses the outward ritual side of religion, answering to "godliness" as the inward. Comp. the cognate word rendered "*worship* of angels" in Col. ii. 18. It is not easy to find an appropriate English adjective for it. "Religious" in its modern sense is too wide, in its old pre-Reformation sense, as meaning one who belonged to a monastic order, too narrow. That sense can hardly be said to have attached to it at the time of the Authorised Version, as the term is used both in the Homilies (e.g. "Christ and his *religion*," Hom. on Holy Scripture) and Bacon's Essays (*Of Unity in Religion*) quite in its modern sense for a whole system of faith and practice. "Devout," "pious," "reverent," suggest themselves, but all fail to express what the Greek beyond question expresses. "Worshipper" would perhaps be the nearest equivalent. "Ritualist," which answers most closely to the strict meaning, has unfortunately acquired a conventional and party meaning.

and bridleth not his tongue] The image was a sufficiently common one in the Greek poets and philosophers. St James returns to it in iii. 2, 3. See note there.

deceiveth his own heart] Here the word is the more common one, as distinguished from that which had been used in verse 22.

27. *Pure religion*] The word still presents the outward aspect of the devout life. Better perhaps, **pure worship**.

undefiled] The term seems chosen with special reference to the Pharisee's scrupulous care to avoid anything that caused ceremonial defilement. Comp. John xviii. 28, "lest they should be *defiled*," where the word is that commonly used in the LXX. for polluted, or being "unclean," as in Lev. v. 3, xi. 23. St James reproduces the teaching of our Lord, that the real defilement comes from within, not from without, that true purity is found in "giving alms of such things as we have" (Mark vii. 20—23, Luke xi. 40).

before God and the Father] The last word seems chosen with a special reference to the duty that follows. We worship the Father when we are like Him in our care for the orphans (Ps. lxviii. 5).

To visit] The Greek word implies somewhat more than that which we commonly attach to the English; "to care for," "look after," as in "God hath *visited* his people" (Luke vii. 16).

the fatherless and widows] These were the natural and therefore proverbial types of extremest affliction. Comp. Job xxix. 12, 13; Ecclus. xxxv. 14. We find from Acts vi. 1, that they occupied a prominent place in what we may venture to call the "Charity Organisation" of the Church of Jerusalem. Comp. also Acts ix. 39; 1 Tim. v. 3—10.

1—13. *Respect of Persons.*

My brethren, have not the faith of our Lord Jesus **2**
Christ, *the Lord* of glory, with respect of persons. For if
there come unto your assembly a man with a gold ring, in

and to keep himself unspotted from the world] The adjective is chosen with special reference to the "undefiled." The "world" is used as including all the circumstances that tempt to sin, especially perhaps, the mass of unrenewed humanity out of which Christians are called, but into which they are in danger of sinking back. The real defilement to be guarded against was to be found in spiritual contact with that "world," and not, as the Pharisee thought, in touching cup or garment that was ceremonially unclean. Comp. chap. iv. 4. In this fullest sense of the word, God alone can thus keep a man unspotted, but it is characteristic of St James to lay stress on the co-operation of man's will, even, we may add, as St Paul does in "keep thyself pure" (1 Tim. v. 22). The teaching of St James finds a striking parallel in that of Philo, who speaks of those who practise "a ritual religion" (using the same word as St James) "instead of holiness" (Philo, p. 173). Comp. also Coleridge, *Aids to Reflection*, Aph. xxiii. "The outward service (θρησκεία) of ancient religion, the rites, ceremonies, and ceremonial vestments of the old law, had morality for their substance. They were the letter of which morality was the spirit; the enigma of which morality was the meaning. But morality itself is the service and ceremonial (*cultus exterior*, θρησκεία) of the Christian religion."

CH. II. 1—13. RESPECT OF PERSONS.

1. *have not the faith...*] Better, **do not hold**. The Greek for "respect of persons" (better, perhaps, **acceptance of persons**) is in the plural, as including all the varied forms in which the evil tendency might shew itself, and stands emphatically immediately after the negative. The name of "our Lord Jesus Christ" is used obviously with a special force. He had shewn Himself, through His whole life on earth, to be no "respecter of persons" (Matt. xxii. 16), to have preferred the poor to the rich. There was a shameful inconsistency when those who professed to hold the faith which had Him as its object acted otherwise. To the name of the Lord Jesus is added the description "*the Lord* of Glory." The first two words are not repeated in the Greek, but the structure of the English sentence requires their insertion. The motive of the addition is clear. In believing in Him who was emphatically a sharer in the Eternal Glory (John xvii. 5), who had now returned to that Glory, men ought to feel the infinite littleness of all the accidents of wealth or rank that separate man from man. This seems the most natural construction, but the position of the words "of glory" is anomalous, and some have joined it with "faith" either as a genitive of the object "faith in the future glory," or as a characterising attribute = "the glorious faith."

2. *if there come unto your assembly*] Literally, **into your synagogue**, the old familiar name as yet, in that early stage of the Church's goodly apparel, and there come in also a poor *man* in vile raiment; and ye have respect to him that weareth the gay clothing, and say unto him, Sit thou here in a good place; life, being used for the Christian as for the Jewish place of worship. What is noted presented the most glaring and offensive form which the acceptance of persons had taken. Signs of the eagerness of men who aimed at a high religious reputation to obtain such honours are seen in Matt. xxiii. 6; and in a society so pervaded by worldliness as that of Judæa, wealth, if accompanied by any kind of religiousness, was sure to be accepted as covering a multitude of sins. What grieved St James was that the same evil should have crept in even among the disciples of the Lord of Glory.

a man with a gold ring] Literally, **a gold-ringed man**, implying, probably, more than one. The custom was one of the fashions of the Empire, and had spread from Rome to Judæa. So Juvenal, in a portrait which unites the two forms of ostentatious luxury noted by St James, describes one who, though born as an Egyptian slave, appears with Tyrian robes upon his shoulders, and golden rings, light or heavy, according to the season (*Sat.* I. 28. 30). So in Martial (XI. 60) we read of one who wears six rings on every finger, day and night, and even when he bathes.

in goodly apparel] Better, **in gorgeous, or bright apparel**. The word is the same as that used of the robe placed upon our Lord in mockery (Luke xxiii. 11), and of that in which the Angel appeared to Cornelius (Acts x. 30). The primary idea is that of "bright" or shining, and this effect was often produced by a combination of gold embroidery with Tyrian purple and crimson.

in vile raiment] **squalid** is perhaps the nearest equivalent to the Greek word. It is used in the LXX. of Zech. iii. 4, of the "filthy garments" of Joshua the High-Priest. In Rev. xxii. 11 it is used of spiritual "filthiness," as is the cognate noun in chap. i. 21 of this Epistle.

3. *And ye have respect to*] Better, **look with respect upon**. The same word is used in Luke i. 48, ix. 38. The English version weakens the dramatic vividness of the Greek.

the gay clothing] The English presents a needless variation from the Greek, which has the same words as in the preceding verse. The translators would seem to have acted on their principle of bringing in as many English words as they could by way of fairness. See *Preface to the Authorised Version.*

Sit thou here in a good place] The English paraphrases the Greek, which runs literally, as in the margin, **Sit here honourably**. In practice the seats most coveted among the Jews were those near the end of the synagogue which looked towards Jerusalem, and at which stood the ark that contained the sacred roll of the Law. We do not know whether the first meeting-places of the Christian society followed the same arrangements, or whether then, as at a later period, the Table of the Lord took the place which had been occupied by the ark, and led them to covet the places that were near it, and therefore well placed for seeing and hearing the officiating elder.

and say to the poor, Stand thou there, or sit here under my footstool: are ye not then partial in yourselves, and are 4 become judges of evil thoughts? Hearken, my beloved 5 brethren, Hath not God chosen the poor of this world rich in faith, and heirs of the kingdom which he hath promised to them that love him? But ye have despised the poor. 6

Stand thou there...] The Christian, probably the elder or deacon, is supposed to point the poor man to his place at the other end of the synagogue, far from sight and hearing, giving him, it may be, the alternative of a seat on the ground, just below what we should call the "stall," in which the rich man was invited to take his place, with a stool for his feet to rest on.

4. *are ye not then partial in yourselves?*] The verb is the same as that translated "waver" in chap. i. 6 and elsewhere, as in Matt. xxi. 21; Mark xi. 23; Acts x. 20; Rom. xiv. 23 by "doubt." Nor is any other meaning, such as that of "making distinctions," necessary, or admissible, here. "When you acted in this way (the tense assumes that the thing had been actually done) did you not *doubt*, as others doubt, in your own hearts?" Faith in Christ's words as to the deceitfulness of riches and the little honour due to them would have kept men from such servility. They shewed by their words and acts that they were half-hearted, or, in St James's sense of the word, "double-minded."

judges of evil thoughts?] The construction is the same as that of the English phrase "a man of bad temper," and is precisely analogous to that rendered "unjust judge" (literally, **judge of injustice**) in Luke xviii. 6, and to the "forgetful hearer" or "hearer of forgetfulness" in chap. i. 25. It means accordingly, "**evil-thinking judges.**" In acting as they did, men made themselves judges between rich and poor, and with "base reasonings," or better, perhaps, what we call "base calculations," gave a preference to the former.

5. *Hath not God chosen...*] Better, perhaps, **did not God choose?** as referring to the special election of the poor by Christ as the heirs of blessings and the messengers of His Kingdom (Matt. v. 3; Luke vi. 20; comp. also 1 Cor. i. 27).

the poor of this world] Literally, **in this world**, i. e. "as far as this world is concerned."

rich in faith] The construction of the words is (to use a technical phrase) that of a secondary predicate, "God had chosen the poor in this world as, i.e. to be, rich in faith, as in the region in which they lived and moved."

heirs of the kingdom which he hath promised...] Here, as before (ch. i. 12), it is scarcely possible to exclude a direct reference to the words of Christ, as in Luke vi. 20, xii. 31, 32, and so we get indirect proof of a current knowledge, at the early period at which St James wrote, of teaching that was afterwards recorded in the written Gospels. Some of the better MSS., however, give "heirs of the promise."

to them that love him?] Care is taken not to lead men to suppose that poverty itself, apart from spiritual conditions, was a sufficient title to the

Do not rich *men* oppress you, and draw you before the
7 judgment seats? Do not they blaspheme *that* worthy name

inheritance. There must be the love of God which has its root in
faith. What is pressed is that poverty and not wealth was the true
object of respect; partly as predisposing men to the spiritual conditions, partly as having been singled out by Christ for special blessings.

6. *But ye have despised the poor*] Better, **ye have dishonoured,
or done dishonour to,** the word implying the outward act that expressed contempt. The Greek tense may point to the special instance just given as a supposed fact, "Ye dishonoured...." The pronoun is emphatic, "God chose the poor, *ye* put them to shame."

Do not rich men oppress you] Better, **lord it over you.** The word is like, though not identical with, those used in Matt. xx. 25 ; 1 Pet. v. 3, and means literally, **to act the potentate over others.** As a rule the wealthier class in Judæa tended to Sadducecism (Joseph. *Ant.* XIII. 10. § 6), and St James's reference to their treatment of the disciples agrees with the part that sect took, including, as it did, the aristocracy of the priesthood, in the persecutions of the earlier chapters of the Acts (iv. 1, 6, v. 17).

and draw you before the judgment seats?] Better, **drag you to courts of justice.** The same noun appears in 1 Cor. vi. 2, 4. The Greek verb implies violence, as in Acts xxi. 30. The words may point either to direct persecutions, such as that of Acts ix. 1, 2, or to the indirect vexation of oppressive lawsuits. In the Greek the verb is preceded by an emphatic pronoun, "Is it not *they* that drag you." There seems, at first, a want of logical coherence. The rich man first appears as gaining undue prominence in the assembly of Christians, and then as one of a class of persecutors and blasphemers. This, however, is just the point on which St James lays stress. Men honoured the rich Christian, not because he was a Christian, but because he was rich, i. e. because he was connected with a class, which, as such, had shewn itself bitterly hostile to them.

7. *Do not they blaspheme that worthy name*] Better, **Do not they revile that noble Name?** The pronoun is again emphatic, **Is it not they that revile?** The two senses of the Greek verb, the reviling which has man for its object, and the blasphemy, in its modern sense, which is directed against God, are in this instance so closely mingled that it is difficult to say which predominates. Men reviled Christ as a deceiver, and in so doing were, not knowing what they did, blaspheming the Son of God. The Name can be none other than that of Jesus as the Christ, and the epithet attached to it, "which *is given you, or called upon you*," is best explained as referring to the name of Christian, which was beginning to spread from Antioch into Palestine (Acts xi. 26). Where it had not yet found its way, it was probable enough that the disciples of Jesus would be known by the name out of which "Christian" sprang, as of Χριστοῦ, "Christ's people," "Christ's followers." The description reminds us of the account St Paul gives of his work in compelling the saints to "blaspheme" (Acts xxvi. 11). The persecution in which he thus took part was instigated, it will be remembered, by the Sadducean

by the which ye are called? If ye fulfil the royal law ac- 8
cording to the scripture, Thou shalt love thy neighbour
as thyself, ye do well : but if ye have respect to persons, ye 9
commit sin, and are convinced of the law as transgressors.
For whosoever shall keep the whole law, and *yet* offend in 10
one *point*, he is guilty of all. For he that said, Do not 11

priests, who formed a wealthy aristocracy, rather than by the more cautious Pharisees, who adopted the policy of Gamaliel (Acts v. 17, 34).
8. *If ye fulfil the royal law according to the scripture*] The Greek gives a particle which is not expressed in the English, "If, however, ye fulfil..." Nothing that the writer has said in disparagement of wealth and the wealthy is to lead men to anything at variance with the great law of love; that law embraces rich and poor alike. The position of the verb in the Greek gives it a special emphasis. The "law" which follows may be called "royal" or "kingly," either (1) in the sense in which Plato speaks (*Minos* II. 566) of a just law as kingly or sovereign, using the same adjective as St James, or (2) as coming from God or Christ as the true King and forming part of the fundamental code of the kingdom. In a Greek writer the first would probably be the thought intended. In one like St James, living in the thought of a Divine kingdom, and believing in Jesus as the King, the latter is more likely to have been prominent. This agrees too more closely with the uniform use of the word in the LXX. in a literal and not a figurative sense. The law which follows, from Lev. xix. 18, had been solemnly affirmed by the true King (Matt. xxii. 39). One who accepted it in its fulness was *ipso facto* not far from the Kingdom (Mark xii. 34). Believing this to have been the main thought present to St James's mind, it is yet probable enough that he chose the word so that those who were not as yet believers in Christ might see in the commandment of love, the law of God as the Great King.

ye do well] The words seem to point to those who, like the scribe in Mark xii. 32, 33, were ready enough to accept the law in theory but shrank from its practical application. We almost trace a tone of irony in the words : "In that case, if you attain a completeness which you never have attained, ye do well." "**Right well**," or "**nobly**," or more colloquially "excellent well," comes closer to the force of the adverb.

9. *but if ye have respect to persons*] The Greek gives a compound verb which is not found elsewhere, **If ye be person-accepting.**

ye commit sin] The Greek is more emphatic, "**It is sin** that ye are working, being convicted by the Law." However generally decorous their lives might be, yet through this one offence they failed to meet the requirements of the Law. The way in which they dealt with rich and poor was, in the strictest sense of the term, a crucial test.

10. *in one point*] The noun, as the italics shew, is not in the Greek, but the English is a satisfactory rendering. Guided by what follows we might perhaps say "in one *commandment*."

he is guilty of all] Better, **he has become guilty**, i. e. liable to con-

commit adultery, said also, Do not kill. Now if thou commit no adultery, yet *if* thou kill, thou art become a trans-
12 gressor of the law. So speak ye, and so do, as they that
13 shall be judged by the law of liberty. For he shall have

demnation under an indictment which includes all the particular commandments included in the great Law. This seems at first of the nature of an ethical paradox, but practically it states a deep moral truth. If we wilfully transgress one commandment we shew that in principle we sit loose to all. It is but accident, or fear, or the absence of temptation, that prevents our transgressing them also. Actual transgression in one case involves potential transgression in all. A saying of Rabbi Jochanan is recorded in the Talmud (*Sabbath*, fol. 70) identical with this in its terms, and including in its range what were classed as the 39 precepts of Moses. St James was urging upon devout Jews, whether they believed in Christ or no, the highest ethical teaching of their own schools. It is probable enough, that the Pharisees who misrepresented the teaching of St James in the Church of Antioch, laid stress on these words as including circumcision and the ceremonial Law, as well as the precepts which were moral and eternal (Acts xv. 1, 5, 24). See *Introduction*, ch. III.

11. *For he that said, Do not commit adultery*...] The two commandments are chosen as standing first in the Second Table, the fifth being classed by most Jewish writers as belonging to the First, just as in Greek and Roman ethics, duty to parents came under the head of Εὐσέβεια and *Pietas*, rather than under that of Justice (comp. 1 Tim. v. 4). This division is recognised by Josephus (*Ant.* III. 6. § 6) and Philo (*De Decal.* 1.), and falls in better than the common one with the *pentad* and *duad* grouping that pervades the Law. It is singular that in all New Testament quotations from the Second Table "Thou shalt not commit adultery" precedes "Thou shalt not kill," Mark x. 19; Luke xviii. 20; Rom. xiii. 9; and the order is made the subject of direct comment by Philo (*De Decal.* XII. 24). It may be inferred from this that there was, probably, a traditional order varying from that at present found in the Hebrew Pentateuch.

12. *So speak ye, and so do*] The thoughts of the teacher dwell, as before (chap. i. 26) and afterwards (chap. iii. 1—12), on sins of speech as no less tests of character than sins of act. In so doing he was echoing the words of a yet greater Teacher (Matt. xii. 37).

the law of liberty] See note on ch. i. 25. The recurrence of the phrase indicates a certain fondness for the thought which it expresses. As a phrase it is peculiar to St James, but the idea is found in John viii. 32. Verbally it presents something like a contrast to St Paul's language as to the law "which gendereth unto bondage" (Gal. iv. 24), but the difference is on the surface only, St James speaking of the moral law when the will accepts it as the guide of life, St Paul of its work as reproving and condemning when the fleshly will resists it, and pre-eminently of its merely ritual and ceremonial precepts, the days and months and years of Gal. iv. 10.

judgment without mercy, that hath shewed no mercy; and mercy rejoiceth against judgment.

14—26. *Justification by Faith and Works.*

What *doth it* profit, my brethren, though a man say *he* 14

13. *For he shall have judgment*] There is something more emphatic in the actual structure of the sentence, **For the judgment shall be merciless to him that wrought not mercy.** The axiom presents one aspect of the great law of divine retribution, and, like so much of St James's teaching, is an obvious reproduction of that of the Sermon on the Mount (Matt. vii. 1). The reference to that discourse suggests the thought that the "law of liberty" of which St James speaks is not the law given by Moses, but the new Law, full of grace and truth, which was given by Christ. See note on verse 8. On this assumption the supposed contrast with St Paul dwindles into nothing.

mercy rejoiceth against judgment] The verb is found in Rom. xi. 18. The abruptness of the original, where the maxim stands with no connecting particle, is singularly forcible, **mercy glories over judgment.** The law holds good universally. It is true of man's judgment, but also of God's, that mercy triumphs over severity, when it finds a willing object. The truth has seldom found a nobler utterance than in the familiar words which remind us that

"Earthly power doth then shew likest God's,
When mercy seasons justice."
SHAKESPEARE. *Merchant of Venice*, IV. 1.

14—26. JUSTIFICATION BY FAITH AND WORKS.

14. *though a man say he hath faith*] The section on which we now enter has been the battle-field of almost endless controversies. It led Luther in the boldness of a zeal not according to knowledge to speak of the whole Epistle with contempt. (*Preface to German New Testament*, 1522; but see J. C. Hare's *Vindication of Luther*, p. 215.) To him it was an "Epistle of Straw," (*Epistola straminea,*) to be classed with wood, hay, stubble, as compared with the teaching of St Paul, which it seemed to him to contradict. It led Bishop Bull to write his *Harmonia Apostolica* to prove the agreement of the two, by assuming, with many of the Fathers, that St James wrote to correct the false inferences which men had drawn from St Paul's doctrine, in itself and as taught by him a true doctrine, as to Justification. In dealing with the problem presented by a comparison of the teaching of the two writers, it is obviously necessary to start with what to the reader is an assumption, though to the writer it may be the conclusion of an inquiry, as to the aim and leading idea of the writer with whom we have to deal; and the notes that follow will accordingly be based on the hypothesis that the teaching of St James was not meant, as men have supposed who exaggerate the diversities of thought in the Apostolic age, to be antagonistic to that of St Paul, nor even to correct mistaken inferences from it, but was altogether inde-

15 hath faith, and have not works? can faith save him? If a
16 brother or sister be naked, and destitute of daily food, and

pendent, and probably prior in time, moving in its own groove, and taking its own line of thought. If this view, as a theory, solves all the phænomena, and throws light upon what would otherwise be obscure, it will be its own best vindication. At the close it may be well to take a brief survey of other modes of interpretation.

We must remember then, to start with, that St James is writing primarily to the Jews of the "dispersion." The disciples in Jerusalem and Judæa were under his personal guidance, and therefore were not in need of an Epistle. The faults which he reproves are pre-eminently the faults of the race. Men dwelling, as those Jews dwelt, in the midst of a heathen population, were tempted to trust for their salvation to their descent from Abraham (comp. Matt. iii. 9) and to their maintaining the unity of the Godhead as against the Polytheism and idolatry of the nations. They repeated their Creed (known, from its first Hebrew word, as the *Shemà*), "Hear, O Israel, the Lord our God is one Lord" (Deut. vi. 4). It entered, as our Creed does, into the Morning and Evening Services of the Synagogue. It was uttered by the dying as a passport to the gates of Paradise. It was to this that they referred the words of Habakkuk that the just should live by faith (Hab. ii. 4). St James saw, as the Baptist had seen before him, how destructive all this was of the reality of the spiritual life, and accordingly takes this as the next topic of his letter.

No emphasis is to be laid on "though a man *say.*" The argument of St James assumes that the man has the faith which he professes. His contention is that faith is not enough by itself, that unless it pass into "works" it gives proof that it is *ipso facto* dead; and the "works" of which he speaks are, as the next verse shews, emphatically, not ceremonial, nor ascetic, but those of an active benevolence.

can faith save him?] The pronoun, and, in the Greek, the article prefixed to faith, are emphatic. " Can his faith save *him*, being such as he is?" There is no slight cast upon faith generally, though the kind of faith in the particular case is declared to be worthless.

15. *If a brother or sister...*] The words are not necessarily used in the sense in which they imply the profession of faith in Christ as they are, e. g., in Acts x. 1; xi. 1; 1 Cor. v. 11. Every Israelite was to see a brother in every child of Abraham (Matt. v. 23; Acts ii. 29, iii. 17). All that can be said is that where the reader of the Epistle was a Christian, he would feel that the words brought before him those who were of the same society or brotherhood.

naked, and destitute of daily food] The picture drawn is one of extremest destitution, and, like the teaching of the whole passage, reminds us of Matt. xxv. 36, 43. What was the faith worth which could witness that suffering and not be stirred to help? The words are applicable to all times and countries, but it gives them a special interest to remember that the Church over which St James presided had suffered, and was probably, at the very time he wrote, suffering, from the famine foretold by Agabus (Acts xi. 28—30). The Gentile disciples had, we read, one of you say unto them, Depart in peace, be *ye* warmed and filled; notwithstanding ye give them not those *things which are* needful to the body; what *doth it* profit? Even 17 so faith, if it hath not works, is dead, *being* alone. Yea, a 18 man may say, Thou hast faith, and I have works: shew me

done their best to alleviate the distress of the Churches of Judæa. St James's language, addressed to the Jews and Jewish Christians of the dispersion, would seem to imply that they had shewn less forwardness, and had wrapt themselves up in the self-satisfaction of professing the orthodox faith of the sons of Abraham, while the Gentile converts whom they despised were setting an example of self-denying charity.

16. *Depart in peace*] The phrase was one of familiar benediction, and had been used by our Lord to those who came to Him seeking bodily or spiritual healing (Luke vii. 50, viii. 48; Acts xvi. 36). It would naturally only be used where such wants, if they existed, had been, or were going to be, relieved.

be ye warmed and filled] The first verb refers obviously to the naked, the second to those who are destitute of food. The Greek verbs may be either in the imperative or indicative, "**Get yourselves warmed and filled**," or "*Ye are warming and filling yourselves.*" The former is the more generally received interpretation, and represents the kind of benevolence which shews itself in good advice. The idea of mere good wishes is excluded by the use, on this assumption, of the imperative. It may perhaps, however, be questioned whether the indicative does not give a preferable meaning. The man whose faith was only the acceptance and the utterance of a dogma, was mocking the souls of others when he said "God is One—God is your Father," as much as if he said to the naked or hungry, "Ye are being warmed or filled." No amount of faith on their part could turn that mockery of a feast into a reality, unless they had the food and clothing they needed; and the man who gave a bare dogma to men without the reality of love, was mocking them,—yes, and cheating himself,—in much the same manner.

notwithstanding ye give them not] Better, **and** *ye give them not*. The change to the plural generalises the individual case presented in "one of you."

17. *Even so faith, if it hath not works*...] This then is St James's objection to the faith of which he speaks. It is, while alone (literally, **by itself**), with no promise or potency of life, and it is, therefore, dead, and being so, as we scarcely call a corpse a man, is unworthy of the name of faith. The assent to a dogma, beginning and ending in itself, has no power to justify or save. St Paul's language in Rom. ii. 13 shews that he was in substantial agreement with St James.

18. *Yea, a man may say*...] The objector thus introduced, after the same manner as by St Paul in 1 Cor. xv. 35, is here the representative neither of an opponent to be refuted, nor yet of the writer's own thoughts, but rather, as we should say, of an outsider, the man of common sense and practical piety, in this instance, of the Gentile convert whom the orthodox Jew or Jewish Christian despised, who

thy faith without thy works, and I will shew thee my faith
19 by my works. Thou believest that there is one God; thou
20 doest well: the devils also believe, and tremble. But wilt
thou know, O vain man, that faith without works is dead?

might be less expert in formulating the Truth, but lived by the Truth
which he believed.

shew me thy faith without thy works] The reading followed by the
English version is at once more intelligible and supported by better MS.
authority, than the alternative "**by** *thy works*," which, in fact, destroys
the whole point of the antithesis. The man who relied on faith is
challenged to exhibit it, if he can, apart from works, as a distinct entity
by itself. It is assumed that no such exhibition is possible. If he is to
give any evidence that he has the faith that saves, it must be by having
recourse to the works which he neglects, and, it may be, disparages.
On the other hand, the challenger, starting with works, can point to them
as proofs of something beyond themselves. Deeds of love, implying a
victory over self, could not have been wrought without, not a dead
faith in the dogma of the Divine Unity, but a living trust in God.

19. *Thou believest that there is one God...*] The instance of the faith
in which men were trusting is important as shewing the class of Soli-
fidians (to use a term which controversy has made memorable) which St
James had in view. They were not those who were believing in the Son of
God, trusting in the love, the blood, in the language of a later age, the
merits, of Christ, but men who, whether nominally Christians or Jews,
were still clinging to their profession of the Creed of Israel as the
ground of all their hopes. It is scarcely probable that a writer in-
tending to correct consequences drawn from St Paul's teaching as to
faith would have been content with such a far-off illustration.

thou doest well] The words have the character of a half-ironical con-
cession. Comp. note on verse 8. It is well as far as it goes, but the
demons can claim the same praise.

the devils also believe and tremble] Better "**shudder.**" The general
bearing of the words is plain enough, but there is a special meaning
which is commonly passed over. The "devils" are the "**demons**"
or "unclean spirits" of the Gospels, thought of, not as in their prison-
house of darkness (Jude *v.* 6), but as "possessing" and tormenting
men. As such, they too acknowledged the Unity and Sovereignty of
God, but that belief, being without love, led only to the "shudder" of
terror, when the Divine Name was uttered in the formulæ of exorcism.
(Comp. Matt. viii. 29; Mark ix. 20, 26.) Here then was an instance in
which belief in a dogma, as distinct from trust in a person, brought
with it no consciousness of peace or pardon, and what was true of the
"demons" might be true also of men.

20. *wilt thou know, O vain man...*] The term, as applied to men, is
not found elsewhere in the New Testament, but is used with something of
the same significance in the LXX. of Judg. ix. 4. The idea is primarily
that of "emptiness," and the Greek adjective is almost literally the

Was not Abraham our father justified by works, when he had 21
offered Isaac his son upon the altar? Seest thou how faith 22
wrought with his works, and by works was faith made perfect?

equivalent of our **empty-headed**, as a term of contempt. It answers clearly to the *Raca* of Matt. v. 22.
that faith without works is dead] The MSS. vary between "dead" and the adjective rendered "idle" in Matt. xii. 36, xx. 3. The meaning is substantially the same. That which is without life is without the activity which is the one proof of life.
21. *Was not Abraham our father justified by works*] The close correspondence of phraseology with Rom. iv. 2 at first seems to favour the view that St James is correcting or modifying St Paul's statement. It is obvious, however, that the agreement equally admits of the explanation that St Paul is correcting or modifying the language of St James. He presses the fact that "Abraham believed God," and that this "was counted to him for righteousness," i.e. that he was justified prior to any act but that of simple trust. And the impression left by a careful study of the passage referred to is that St Paul is there referring to something that had been urged, as having a high authority, against his teaching that a man is justified by faith. It is clear, at all events, that no inference can be drawn from the two passages in favour of the assumption that the Epistle of St James was later than that of St Paul to the Romans.
The use of the word "justify" shews that its meaning is to "acquit" or "count as righteous" (Matt. xii. 37; Acts xiii. 39; Ecclus. xxvi. 29, xxiii. 11).
The preposition used in the Greek points to "works" as being the source rather than the instrument of justification.
when he had offered Isaac his son upon the altar?] Better, **when he offered Isaac**, the two acts being thought of, not as successive, but simultaneous. It is remarkable that the only scriptural references, after Gen. xxii., to the sacrifice of Isaac, are found in Wisd. x. 5 and Heb. xi. 17. It is hardly likely that the latter could have been known to St James, the internal evidence pointing to a later date; but the former, whether, as some have supposed, by the same author as the Epistle to the Hebrews, or written fifty or sixty years earlier, might well have come under his notice. In relation to St Paul's teaching, as noticed above, it must be remembered that the one writer speaks of the beginning of Abraham's course, the other of its consummation. St James might well urge that if Abraham had not shewn his faith by his works, up to the crowning work of the sacrifice of his son, it would have proved that his faith too was dead.
22. *Seest thou how faith wrought with his works...?*] Better, perhaps, not as a question, **Thou seest that**... Attention is called, not as the English "how" suggests, to the manner of co-operation, but only to the fact. The tense of the verb emphasises the continued co-operation of Abraham's faith with his works. The one was all along working together with the other. What St James presses is, not

23 And the scripture was fulfilled which saith, Abraham believed God, and it was imputed unto him for righteousness: and he was called the Friend of God. 24 Ye see then how that by works a man is justified, and not

that works can justify without faith, but that faith cannot justify unless it includes "the promise and the potency" of the life that shews itself in acts.

by works was faith made perfect?] Here the tense is changed to that which denotes completion in a single act. It was "by works" (i. e. *out of*, as from the originating cause) that faith was brought to its completion. The interpretation which sees in the words nothing more than that faith was shewn to be perfect, must be rejected as one of the afterthoughts of controversy. It may be added, however, as pointing to the true reconciliation of St James and St Paul, that the very form of the statement implies that the faith existed prior to the works by which it was made perfect.

23. *And the scripture was fulfilled*...] The use of the words commonly applied to the fulfilment of prophetic utterances implies that St James saw in the statement of Gen. xv. 6 that which, though true at the time, was yet also an anticipation of what was afterwards to be realised more fully. Of that prophecy, as of others, there were, to use Bacon's phrase, "springing and germinant accomplishments." What was then **reckoned as righteousness** continued to be reckoned, as with an ever-increasing value, which reached its *maximum* in the sacrifice of the son who was the heir of the promise.

and he was called the Friend of God] The words seem to refer, in the English version of the Bible, to 2 Chron. xx. 7 and Isai. xli. 8, where the term "my friend" is applied to Abraham by Jehovah. Singularly enough, however, the term is not found in the Hebrew, nor in the LXX. version, with which St James, writing in Greek, must have been familiar, and which gives, in the first of the two passages, "Abraham thy beloved," and in the second, "whom I loved." The distinctive title first appears in Philo's citation of Gen. xviii. 1 (*De resipisc. Noë*, c. 11), and, after St James, in Clement of Rome (*Epist. ad Cor.* I. 10). It was probably the current phrase in the Jewish schools, and has descended to the Arabs, with whom the name of *El Khalil Allah* (the friend of God), or more briefly *El Khalil*, has practically superseded that of Abraham. Even Hebron, as the city of Abraham, and so identified with him, has become *El Khalil*, "the friend."

24. *Ye see then*] The better MSS. omit the *then*. The Greek verb may be indicative, imperative, or interrogative. The English Version is probably right in giving the preference to the first.

not by faith only] There is, it is obvious, a verbal contradiction between this and St Paul's statement in Rom. iii. 28, but it is verbal only. St James does not exclude faith from the work of justifying, i. e. winning God's acquittal and acceptance, but only a faith which stands "**by itself**," "**alone**," and therefore "**dead**," and assumes that "works" have their beginning in the faith which they ripen and com-

by faith only. Likewise also was not Rahab the harlot 25
justified by works, when she had received the messengers,

plete. St Paul throughout assumes that faith will work by love and be
productive in good acts, while the works which he excludes from the
office of justifying are "works of the law," i.e. works which, whether
ceremonial or moral, are done as by a constrained obedience to an
external commandment, through fear of punishment, or hope of reward,
and are not the spontaneous outcome of love and therefore of faith. It
will be felt that St James presents the more practical, St Paul the
deeper and more mystical aspect of the Truth, and this is in itself a
confirmation of the view maintained throughout these notes, that the
latter was the later of the two, and therefore that so far as one corrects
or completes the popular version of the teaching of the other, it was to
St Paul and not to St James that that task was assigned.

25. *was not Rahab the harlot*...] The question meets us, What led
St James to select this example? St Paul does not refer to it, as he
probably would have done, had he been writing with St James's
teaching present to his thoughts, in any of the Epistles in which
his name appears as the writer. In the Epistle to the Hebrews
(xi. 31) it appears as one of the examples of faith, but this was most
probably after St James had given prominence to her name. In
the mention of Rahab by Clement of Rome (I. 12) we have an obvious
echo from the Epistle just named, with the additional element of
a typical interpretation of the scarlet thread as the symbol of the
blood of Christ, by which those of all nations, even the harlots and
the unrighteous, obtained salvation. A more probable explanation is
found in the connexion of St James with the Gospel according to St
Matthew. The genealogy of the Christ given in ch. i. of that Gospel
must have been known to "the brother of the Lord," and in it the
name of Rahab appeared as having married Salmon, the then "prince"
of the tribe of Judah (Matt. i. 5; 1 Chron. ii. 50, 51; Ruth iv. 20, 21).
The prominence thus given to her name would naturally lead him and
others to think of her history and ask what lessons it had to teach them.
If "harlots" as well as "publicans" were among those who listened to
the warnings of the Baptist and welcomed the gracious words of Christ
(Matt. xxi. 31, 32), she would come to be regarded as the typical representative of the class, the Magdalene (to adopt the common, though, it
is believed, an erroneous view) of the Old Testament. A rabbinic
tradition makes her become the wife of Joshua and the ancestress of eight
distinguished priests and prophets, ending in Huldah the Prophetess
(2 Kings xxii. 14). Josephus (*Ant.* v. 1. § 2), after his manner, tones
down the history, and makes her simply the keeper of an inn. Another
ground of selection may well have been that Rahab was by her position
in the history the first representative instance of the deliverance of one
outside the limits of the chosen people. In this instance also, St James
urges, the faith would have been dead had it been only an assent to
the truth that the God of Israel was indeed God, without passing into
action. The "messengers" are described in Josh. vi. 23 as "young
men," in Heb. xi. 31 as "spies".

26 and had sent *them* out another way? For as the body without the spirit is dead, so faith without works is dead also.

26. *For as the body without the spirit is dead...*] Some MSS. omit the conjunction, but the evidence for retaining it preponderates. The reasoning seems to refer Rahab's justification by works to the wider law that faith without works is dead (as in verse 17) and therefore cannot justify. Our usual mode of thought would lead us to speak of works, the outward visible acts, as the body, and of faith as the spirit or vivifying principle. From St James's standpoint, however, faith "by itself" was simply the assent of the intellect to a dogma or series of dogmas, and this seemed to him to be "dead" until it was vitalised by love shewing itself in act. St Paul reproves the deadness of mere morality, St James that of mere orthodoxy. St James, it will be noted, adopts the simple division of man's nature into "body and spirit," rather than St Paul's more philosophical trichotomy of "body, soul and spirit." 1 Thess. v. 23. Comp. note on ch. iii. 13.

faith without works] More literally, *faith* **apart from** *works*.

ON THE TEACHING OF ST PAUL AND ST JAMES.

The view which has been given in the notes seems to the writer clear and coherent in itself, consistent with what we know as to the relations between the two Apostles, and involving less violence of interpretation than any other hypothesis. Two other views have, however, been maintained with arguments more or less plausible, and it will be well to notice them briefly.

(1) There is the position assumed by some of the bolder critics of the French and German Schools, that there was a real antagonism in the Apostolic Church, not only between the Judaizing teachers and St Paul, but between that Apostle and the three, Peter, James, and John, to whom the Church of the Circumcision looked as its natural leaders. On this assumption, the writer of the Acts of the Apostles strives to gloss over the divergence of the two parties, and to represent an unreal unity. The messages to the Seven Churches are "a cry of passionate hate against St Paul and his followers" (Renan, *St Paul*, p. 367). When St James says, "Wilt thou know, O vain man, that faith without works is dead," he is probably pointing at St Paul himself. From the point of view of those who hold this theory it is, perhaps, a small thing that it is inconsistent with the belief that the teaching of St James and of St Paul had, as its source, the inspiration of the Eternal Spirit, who, though working in many different ways and with wide diversity of gifts, is yet the Spirit of the Truth which is essentially one. But on simply historical grounds the theory is, it is believed, untenable. St Paul himself acknowledges that after he had privately laid before them the sum and substance of the Gospel as he preached it, James, Cephas, and John gave to him the right hands of fellowship (Gal. ii. 9). James appears as giving a public sanction to that Gospel at the Council at Jerusalem (Acts xv. 13—21). Long after

the Judaizing teachers had been doing their worst for years, the "right hand of fellowship" is still held out by the one teacher to the other (Acts xxi. 17—25). The question whether this hypothesis is as satisfactory an explanation of the facts with which it deals, as that which I have here given, I am content to leave to the judgment of the reader.

(2) The other theory has at least the merit of accepting the teaching of each of the two writers as in itself inspired and true. It assumes that St James wrote after St Paul, and aimed at correcting inferences that had been wrongly drawn from his doctrine, that a man is justified by faith without the deeds of the law. How to reconcile their statements on this assumption is a problem which has been variously solved. (*a*) It has been said that St Paul speaks of man's justification before God, St James of the proof of that justification before the eyes of men; but of this there is not a shadow of proof in the language of either writer. (*b*) It has been maintained that St Paul speaks of a true faith, St James of that which is false or feigned; but nothing in the language of the latter, though he stigmatizes the faith which is without works as dead, suggests the thought that it did not mean a real acceptance of the dogma which it professed to hold. (*c*) It has been held that the "works" of which St Paul speaks as unable to justify, are the ceremonial works of the law of Moses, those on which the Pharisees laid stress; but the width of St Paul's teaching as to the nature and office of the law in Gal. iii., Rom. vii. scatters this view to the winds at once. (*d*) There is a nearer approximation to the truth in the solution which finds in St James's faith the intellectual acceptance of a dogma, in St Paul's the trust in a living Person as willing and able to save, and therefore the confidence that salvation is attainable by him who so trusts. This is, in the main, the view that has been taken in these notes, with the exception of the point on which stress has been laid above, that the Antinomianism which St James condemned was that of ultra-Jewish teachers, who taught a justification by faith in Monotheism, and not of an ultra-Pauline party. It agrees practically with the distinction drawn by the Schoolmen that St James speaks of a *fides informis*, rudimentary and incomplete, St Paul of a *fides formata*, developed or completed by Love. Errors, however, assume subtle disguises. Those who used St James's name in the Apostolic age dwelt so much on outward acts apart from the motive that gives them life, as sufficient for man's acceptance with God, that it was necessary for St Paul to revive the truth which had been first distorted and then denied, that "the just by faith shall live" (Hab. ii. 4; Rom. i. 17; Gal. iii. 11). His teaching again, in its turn, led men to think that they might be justified by faith, not in God who justifies, but in a dogma about justification. It was well that both aspects of the truth should have been presented then, and have been preserved for the guidance of the Church in all ages, as completing each the other. We need not fear to be as varied in our teaching as were those who were taught of God, and to tell men, according to their variations in character, as they require more deepening of the spiritual life, or more strengthening for practical activity, now that they must be justified by faith, and now that they must be justified by works.

1—12. *Sins of Speech, and their condemnation.*

3 My brethren, be not many masters, knowing that we
2 shall receive the greater condemnation. For *in* many *things*
we offend all. If any *man* offend not in word, the same *is* a
3 perfect man, *and* able also to bridle the whole body. Behold, we put bits in the horses' mouths, that they may obey
4 us; and we turn about their whole body. Behold also the

CH. III. 1—12. SINS OF SPEECH, AND THEIR CONDEMNATION.

1. *be not many masters*] Better, "*do not* become, or do not get into the way of being *many* teachers." The English word "master," though perhaps conveying the idea of a "schoolmaster" in the sixteenth century, and therefore used in all the versions from Wycliffe and Tyndale onward, is now far too general in its meaning. What St James warns his "brethren" against is each man's setting himself up to be a *teacher*, and in this he echoes our Lord's command, (Matt. xxiii. 8—10). In the Christian Church, as in the Jewish, there was the peril of a self-appointed Rabbi-ship. The sages of Israel had given the same caution, as in the maxim, Love the work, but strive not after the honour, of a Teacher, (*Pirke Aboth*, I. 10).

knowing that we shall receive the greater condemnation] The change from the second person to the first is characteristic of the writer's profound humility. He will not give others a warning without at the same time applying it to himself. The Greek word for "condemnation", though literally meaning "judgment" only, is yet almost always used in the New Testament for an adverse judgment, (e. g. Matt. xxiii. 14; Rom. ii. 2, xiii. 2; 1 Cor. xi. 29, 34). The very form of St James's phrase is as an echo of our Lord's words in the first of the passages referred to.

2. *we offend all*] The word is the same as that in ch. ii. 10. See note there.

a perfect man...] One who has attained the fulness of moral growth, as in 1 Cor. xiv. 20, Heb. v. 14, the same word denotes that of physical growth. Control of speech is named, not as in itself constituting perfection, but as a crucial test indicating whether the man has or has not attained unto it.

able also to bridle the whole body] St James returns to the besetting sin of those to whom he writes, uses the same phrase as in ch. i. 26, and then proceeds to develope the metaphor which it suggests. The "whole body" is used to sum up the aggregate of all the temptations which come to us through the avenues of sense.

3. *Behold, we put bits in the horses' mouths*] The thought of man's power over brute creatures and natural forces, and of his impotence in the greater work of self-government, present a singular parallelism to that of the well-known chorus in the *Antigone* of Sophocles. (332—350):

ships, which though they be so great, and are driven of fierce winds, *yet* are they turned about with a very small helm, whithersoever the governor listeth. Even so the tongue is 5 a little member, and boasteth great things. Behold, how

> Many the forms of life
> Full marvellous in might,
> But man supreme stands out
> Most marvellous of all.
> * * * * * *
> He with the wintry gales,
> O'er the foam-crested sea,
> 'Mid wild waves surging round,
> Tracketh his way across.
> * * * * * *
> He fastens firm the yoke
> On horse with shaggy mane,
> Or bull that walks untamed upon the hills.

So in another passage of the same drama:

> "And I have known the steeds of fiery mood
> With a small curb subdued." (*Antig.* 475.)

4. *Behold also the ships...*] General as the thought is, we may perhaps connect it, as we have done ch. i. 6, with personal recollections of storms on the Galilean lake. It will be seen that this also has its counterpart in Sophocles. The two images are brought together by a writer more within St James's reach than the Greek tragedian. With Philo, Reason in man, the Divine Word in Creation, are compared both with the charioteer and the pilot. (*De Conf. ling.* p. 336. *De Abr.* p. 360). In the latter the very word which St James uses for "governor" is employed also by Philo. The same thoughts appear in the beautiful hymn of Clement of Alexandria as describing the work of Christ as the true Teacher. (*Paedag. ad fin.*):

> "Curb for the stubborn steed
> Making its will give heed.
> * * * * *
> Helm of the ships that keep
> Their pathway o'er the deep.

whithersoever the governor listeth] Better, *the* **pilot or steersman.** This, which, the reader will hardly need to be reminded, is the primary meaning of "governor", has, in the modern use of the word, all but dropped out of sight. Literally the sentence runs, **whithersoever the impulse of the steersman may wish.**

5. *and boasteth great things*] The Greek verb is a compound word, which does not occur elsewhere, but is used not unfrequently by Philo. The fact is not without interest, as indicating, together with

6 great a matter a little fire kindleth. And the tongue *is* a fire, a world of iniquity : so is the tongue amongst our mem-

the parallelisms just referred to, St James's probable acquaintance with that writer.

how great a matter a little fire kindleth] The form of the Greek is somewhat more emphatic. **A little fire kindles how great a mass of timber.** The word translated "matter" means primarily "a forest—wood in growth;" and with this meaning, which is adopted in the Vulgate "*silvam*", the illustration would stand parallel to Homer's simile :

> "As when a spark scarce seen will set ablaze
> The illimitable forest." *Iliad* II. 455.

So in Virgil, *Georg.* II. 303, we have a fuller description of the spark which, dropped at hazard, kindles the bark, and the branches, and the foliage :

> "And as in triumph seizes on the boughs,
> And reigns upon the throne of pine-tree tops,
> And wraps the forest in a robe of flame."

The word, however, had gradually passed into the hands of the metaphysicians, and like the Latin *materia*, which originally meant "timber" (a meaning still traceable in the name of Madeira, "the *well-timbered* island "), had come to mean matter as distinct from form, and then passing back, with its modified meaning, into common use, had been used for a pile, or heap of stuff, or materials of any kind. On the whole then, while admitting the greater vividness of the Homeric similitude, St James is likely to have meant a mass of materials rather than a forest. Comp. Prov. xvi. 27, and Ecclus. xxviii. 10, where we have exactly the same comparison. The Authorised Version may be accordingly received as not far wrong. Here again it may be noted that Philo employs the same similitude to illustrate the growth of goodness in the soul : "As the smallest spark will, if duly fanned, kindle a vast pyre, so is the least element of virtue capable of growth till the whole nature of the man glows with a new warmth and brightness," (Philo, *de Migr. Abr.* p. 407). But he also frequently uses the comparison in reference to the rapid extension of evil.

6. *And the tongue is a fire, a world of iniquity*] The last words are in apposition with the subject, not the predicate, of the sentence. The tongue is described as emphatically **that world**—we should perhaps say, that *microcosm*—**of unrighteousness.** As uttering all evil thoughts and desires, no element of unrighteousness was absent from it, and that which includes all the elements of anything well deserves the name of being its *Cosmos*.

so is the tongue among our members] The particle of comparison is not found in the best MSS., but is clearly implied, and is therefore legitimately inserted in the translation, as it is in some later MSS. The sentence strictly runs, *The tongue* **is set** *in our members*,

bers, that it defileth the whole body, and setteth on fire the course of nature; and it is set on fire of hell. For every 7 referring of course not to a Divine appointment, but to its actual position. It is, as a fact, that which "defiles", better perhaps **spots or stains**, the whole body. Every evil word is thought of as leaving its impress, it may be an indelible impress, as a blot upon the whole character.

and setteth on fire the course of nature] The last words have no parallel in any Greek author, and are therefore naturally somewhat difficult. Literally, we might render, **the wheel of nature** or **of birth**, just as in ch. i. 23 we found "the face of nature," for the "natural face," that with which we are born. The best interpretation seems to be that which sees in the phrase a figure for "the whole of life from birth;" the wheel which then begins to roll on its course, and continues rolling until death. The comparison of life to a race, or course of some kind, has been familiar to the poetry of all ages, and in a Latin poet, Silius Italicus (VI. 120), we have a phrase almost identical with St James's,

"Talis lege Deûm clivoso tramite vitæ
Per varios præceps casus *rota* volvitur *ævi*."

"So by the law of God, through chance and change,
The wheel of life rolls down the steep descent."

What is meant, if we adopt this view, is that from the beginning of life to its close, the tongue is an ever-present inflammatory element of evil.

As an alternative explanation it is possible that there may be a reference to the potter's wheel, as in Jerem. xviii. 3, and Ecclus. xxxviii. 29, in the latter of which the same word for "wheel" is used. On this view the tongue would be represented as the flame that by its untempered heat mars the vessel in the hands of the potter. The frequent parallelisms between St James and the Wisdom of the Son of Sirach, are, as far as they go, in favour of this view, but the former seems to me, on the whole, preferable. A third view, that the words have the same kind of meaning as *orbis terrarum*, and mean, as in the English Version, the whole order or course of nature, i. e. of human history in the world at large, has, it is believed, less to recommend it.

and it is set on fire of hell] The Greek participle is in the present. *The tongue that speaks evil is ever* **being set on fire of Gehenna.** St James does not shrink from tracing sins of speech to their source. The fire of man's wrath is kindled from beneath, as the fire that cleanses is kindled from above. Bearing in our minds the wonder of the day of Pentecost, it is hardly too bold to say that we have to choose whether our tongue shall be purified by the fire of the Holy Spirit or defiled by that of Gehenna. The latter word is that employed in the Gospels, as here, for "Hell", wherever that word means, not simply the place of the dead, which is expressed in the Greek

kind of beasts, and of birds, and of serpents, and of *things*
8 in the sea, is tamed, and hath been tamed of mankind : but
the tongue can no man tame; *it is* an unruly evil, full of
9 deadly poison. Therewith bless we God, even the Father;

by Hades, the unseen world, but the place of torment. Primarily, the word is a Hebrew one, signifying the Valley of Hinnom. As that valley had been in the days of the idolatries of Judah the scene of the fires of Moloch worship (2 Kings xxiii. 10; Jerem. vii. 31, xix. 5, 6), and had in later times become the *cloaca* where the filth and offal of the city were consumed in fires kept continually burning (so it is commonly said, but the fact is not quite certain), it came to be among the later Rabbis what Tartarus was to the Greeks, the symbol of the dread penalties of evil. Comp. Matth. v. 22, Mark ix. 43.

7. *every kind of beasts*] Better, **Every nature.** This was, probably, intended by the translators, as being the old meaning of the word "kind," as in the "kindly fruits" (= "natural products") of the Litany. So Chaucer, "A beautie that cometh not *of kinde*," *Rom. of Rose*, 2288, i. e. that is not natural. It may be noted that the Authorised Version in this instance returns to Wycliffe, who used the word in its old sense, and that all the intermediate versions give "nature." The fourfold classification is obviously intended to be exhaustive—and "beasts" must therefore be taken in its common familiar meaning of "quadruped."

serpents] is too specific for the third word, and it would be better to give the rendering which it commonly has elsewhere, of "creeping things."

is tamed, and hath been tamed of mankind] Better, the word being the same as in the first clause, "**by the nature of man.**" The tense of the first verb implies "**is continually being tamed.**" The assertion may seem at first somewhat hyperbolical, but the well-known cases of tame rats and tame wasps, the lion of Androcles and the white fawn of Sertorius, furnish what may well be termed "crucial instances" in support of it. The story related by Cassian (*Coll.* XXIV. 2), that St John in his old age kept a tame partridge, makes it probable that St James may have seen, among his fellow-teachers, such an instance of the power of man to tame the varied forms of animal life around him.

8. *but the tongue can no man tame*] There is a special force in the Greek tense for "tame", which expresses not habitual, but momentary action. St James had learnt, by what he saw around him, and yet more, it may be, by personal experience, that no powers of the "nature of man" were adequate for this purpose. He had learnt also, we must believe, that the things which are impossible with man are possible with God.

an unruly evil] Literally, **uncontrollable.** Many of the better MSS., however, give the adjective which is rendered "unstable" in ch. i. 8, and which carries with it, together with that meaning, the idea of restlessness and turbulence. So in the *Shepherd* of Hermas (II. 2) calumny is described as a "*restless* demon."

full of deadly poison] Literally, **death-bringing.** For the idea comp.

and therewith curse we men, which are made after the similitude of God. Out of the same mouth proceedeth blessing and cursing. My brethren, these *things* ought not so to be. Doth a fountain send forth at the same place sweet water and bitter? Can the fig tree, my brethren, bear olive berries? either a vine, figs? so *can* no fountain *both* yield salt water and fresh.

"the poison of asps is under their lips," Ps. cxl. 3. The adjective is found in the LXX. version of Job xxxiii. 23, for "angels or messengers of death."

9. *Therewith bless we God, even the Father...*] Many of the better MSS. give "the Lord" instead of "God". The fact dwelt on comes in to illustrate the strange inconsistency, even of men who professed faith in God, in their use of speech. General as the words are, they pointed, we may believe, especially to the feelings of Jews towards Christians, or of the more bigoted section of Jewish Christians towards the Gentiles. Such men were loud in their benedictions of the Eternal, the Blessed One, yet they had not learnt to reverence humanity as such, as made after the likeness of God. They cursed those who worshipped or believed after a different manner from their own. The annals of Christendom shew that the necessity for the warning has not passed away. Councils formulating the faith, and uttering their curses on heretics; *Te Deums* chanted at an *Auto da Fé*, or after a Massacre of St Bartholomew, the railings of religious parties who are restrained from other modes of warfare, present the same melancholy inconsistency.

10. *these things ought not so to be*] The verb, strictly speaking, denotes not so much a state, as the coming into a state: *these things ought not to occur in this way.*

11. *Doth a fountain*] The Greek gives the article, **the fountain,** as more emphatically generalising the truth.

send forth at the same place...] Both verb and noun in the Greek are more vivid. Our word **spurt** or **gush,** if it could be used transitively, would answer to the former; our **mouth,** or "source", or "orifice", to the latter. The comparison was a natural one in a country like Palestine, where springs more or less salt or sulphureous are not uncommon. Most of those on the eastern slope of the hill-country of Judah and Benjamin are indeed brackish. Comp. the sweetening of the spring which supplied the college of the Sons of the Prophets in 2 Kings, ii. 19, and the symbolic healing of the waters in Ezek. xlvii. 9.

12. *Can the fig tree, my brethren, bear olive berries?...*] The comparison here also has an eminently local character. The court-yard of wellnigh every house had its vine and fig-tree (2 Kings xviii. 31). The Mount of Olives supplied the other feature. The idea, as a whole, is parallel to that of Matt. vii. 16, 17, and may well have been suggested by it.

so can no fountain both yield salt water and fresh] The better MSS. give a somewhat briefer form, **Neither can a salt** (spring) **yield sweet**

13—18. *The false Wisdom and the true.*

13 Who *is* a wise *man* and endued with knowledge amongst you? let him shew out of a good conversation his works 14 with meekness of wisdom. But if ye have bitter envying

(the same adjective as in the preceding verse) **water.** The comparison seems at first to break down, as the fact which it was meant to illustrate was that "blessing and cursing" did issue from the same mouth. What is meant, however, is that in such a case, the "blessing" loses its character, and is tainted with the bitterness of the cursing. The prayers and praises of the hypocrite who cherishes hatred in his heart, are worse than worthless.

13—18. THE FALSE WISDOM AND THE TRUE.

13. *Who is a wise man and endued with knowledge among you?*] The adjective corresponding to "endued with knowledge" (literally **knowing** or *understanding*) is not found elsewhere in the New Testament, but occurs in the LXX. of Deut. i. 13, 15; iv. 6; Isai. v. 21. So far as a distinction is intended, it expresses the intellectual, as "wise" does the moral, aspect of wisdom. Both qualities were required in one who claimed to be, as in verse 1, a "Master" or "Teacher," and St James, in strict sequence of thought, proceeds to point out how the conditions may be fulfilled.

out of a good conversation] The tendency of modern usage to restrict the meaning of the substantive to "talk" is in this instance, where the immediate context suggests some such meaning, specially unfortunate, as lowering the range of the precept. Better **by,** or *out of,* **his good** (the word expresses the *nobler* form of goodness) **conduct.** Comp. the use of the word in Gal. i. 13; 1 Pet. i. 15, 18, and elsewhere.

with meekness of wisdom] Better, **in** *meekness,* as expressing not something super-added, but the very form and manner in which the *noble conduct* was to be shewn. The "meekness" thus defined is thought of as belonging to "wisdom" as its characteristic attribute. St James is hence led back to the thought with which the Epistle opened, that wisdom is the crown and consummation of the character of a true believer; and lest a counterfeit wisdom should be taken for the true, he proceeds to give the notes of difference between them.

14. *But if ye have bitter envying and strife in your hearts*] Better, *envy and* **rivalry.** The latter substantive, formed from a word which means a "day-labourer", expresses primarily the temper of competition that characterised the class, and then more generally, faction and party-spirit of any kind. It is significant that the word for "envy" is used by St Luke as specially characterising the temper of the Jews towards the Gentile converts (Acts xiii. 45), and this, together with what we have seen of the true bearing of ch. ii. 14—26, leads to the conclusion that St James's warning is specially addressed to those of the Circumcision who displayed that feeling. He is shewing himself not the antagonist,

and strife in your hearts, glory not, and lie *not* against the truth. This wisdom descendeth not from above, 15 but *is* earthly, sensual, devilish. For where envying and 16

but the supporter of St Paul's work, condemning the factious spirit which was then, as afterwards, at Corinth (2 Cor. xii. 20), in Galatia (Gal. v. 20), and at Rome (Phil. i. 15), his chief hindrance. The word "bitter" is perhaps added to "envy" because the Greek word "zeal" was neutral, and admitted of a good meaning.

glory not] The word expresses a relative, not an absolute glorying, a glorying **over** some one, on the ground of superior privileges. This was, it is obvious, likely to be the besetting sin of the party of the Circumcision in relation to the Gentiles, and was therefore checked by St James, just as afterwards, when the prospect of the rejection of Israel was becoming a certainty, it became, in its turn, the sin of the Gentile converts, and was then checked by St Paul (Rom. xi. 18).

lie not against the truth] It is clear that if the word "truth" were only subjective in its meaning, as meaning "truthfulness," the precept would be open to the charge of tautology. We must therefore assume that it is used with an objective force, as the truth of God revealed in Christ. We ask what special truth thus revealed those to whom St James wrote were most in danger of denying, and the answer lies on the surface. They were claiming God as the God of the Jews only (Rom. iii. 29), denying the brotherhood of mankind in Christ, "lying against" the very truth of which they fancied that they were the exclusive possessors.

16. *This wisdom descendeth not from above*] St James returns to the thought of chap. i. 5, that true wisdom was the gift of God, coming, like every other good and perfect gift, from above (ch. i. 17). But this was not "the wisdom" of which the "many teachers" of the party of the Circumcision were boasting. It was, however, that of the Proverbs of Solomon, and of the Wisdom of the Son of Sirach, on which so much of St James's teaching was modelled. (Comp. Ecclus. i. 1—10.) It was that which had been manifested to mankind in all its fulness in Christ.

earthly, sensual, devilish] Each word is full of meaning. (1) The counterfeit wisdom is "earthly" in its nature and origin as contrasted with that which cometh from above. (Comp. St Paul's "who mind *earthly* things," Phil. iii. 19). (2) It is "sensual." The word is used by classical writers for that which belongs to the "soul" as contrasted with the "body." This rested on the twofold division of man's nature. The psychology of the New Testament, however, assumes generally the threefold division of body, soul, and spirit, the second element answering to the animal, emotional life, and the third being that which includes reason and will, the capacity for immortality and for knowing God. Hence the adjective formed from "soul" acquired a lower meaning, almost the very opposite of that which it once had, and expresses man's state as left to lower impulses without the control of the spirit. So St Paul contrasts the *natural* man with the spiritual

17 strife *is*, there *is* confusion and every evil work. But the wisdom that is from above is first pure, then peaceable, gentle, *and* easy to be intreated, full of mercy and good

(1 Cor. ii. 14), the *natural* and the spiritual body (1 Cor. xv. 44, 46). So St Jude describes the false teachers, whom he condemns as "*sensual*, having not the Spirit." What St James says then of the false wisdom is that it belongs to the lower, not the higher, element in man's nature. It does not come from the Spirit of God, and therefore is not spiritual. (3) In "devilish" we have yet a darker condemnation. Our English use of the same word, "devil," for the two Greek words *diabolos* and *dæmonion*, tends, however, to obscure St James's meaning. The epithet does not state that the false wisdom which he condemns came from *the* devil, or was like his nature, but that it was **demon-like**, as partaking of the nature of the "demons" or "unclean spirits," who, as in the Gospels, are represented as possessing the souls of men, and reducing them to the level of madness. Such, St James says, is the character of the spurious wisdom of the "many masters" of verse 1. Met together in debate, wrangling, cursing, swearing, one would take them for an assembly of demoniacs. Their disputes were marked by the ferocity, the egotism, the boasting, the malignant cunning of the insane. St Paul's account of the "doctrines of devils," i. e. proceeding from demons (1 Tim. iv. 1), not from the Spirit of God, presents a striking parallel. St James's previous allusion to "demons" (see note on ch. ii. 19) confirms the interpretation thus given, as shewing how much his thoughts had been directed to the phænomena of possession.

16. *envying and strife*] Better, as before, **envy and rivalry**. See note on verse 14.

there is confusion and every evil work] On the first word see note on verse 8. It describes here the chaotic turbulence of such an assembly as that indicated in the preceding verse. Comp. Prov. xxvi. 28, where the Greek word in the LXX. answers to the "ruin" of the English version. The word for "evil" is not the common one, and expresses contempt as well as condemnation. Better, **every vile deed**. It is the word used in John iii. 20, v. 29.

17. *But the wisdom that is from above is first pure, then peaceable*] The sequence is that of thought, not of time. It is not meant, i. e. that purity is an earlier stage of moral growth in wisdom than peace, but that it is its foremost attribute. The "purity" indicated is especially that of chastity of flesh and spirit (comp. 2 Cor. vii. 11, xi. 2; Tit. ii. 5), and as such is contrasted with the "sensual" character of the false wisdom. Here again we have the tone of one who has learnt from the Masters of those who know, among the teachers of his own people, that wisdom will not "dwell in the body that is subject unto sin" (Wisd. i. 4). The sequence which places "peaceful" after "pure" has its counterpart in the beatitudes of the Sermon on the Mount (Matt. v. 8, 9).

gentle, and easy to be intreated] The word for "gentle" means literally, **forbearing**. It describes, as in Aristotle (*Eth.* x. 6), the temper that does not press its rights, that is content to suffer wrong (comp. Phil. iv.

fruits, without partiality, and without hypocrisy. And the 18 fruit of righteousness is sown in peace of them that make peace.

5; 1 Tim. iii. 3). The second adjective is used by classical writers, both in a passive sense as here, and active, (1) as meaning "persuasive," "winning its way by gentleness," or (2) as "obedient." Our choice between the three meanings must depend on our view of what is most likely to have been the sequence of St James's thoughts. On the whole, the second seems to me to have the most to commend it. True wisdom shews itself, St James seems to say, in that subtle yet gentle power to persuade and win, which we all feel when we come in contact with one who is clearly not fighting for his own rights, but for the cause of Truth.

full of mercy and good fruits] The train of thought is carried on. Wisdom is suasive because she is compassionate. In dealing with the froward she is stirred, not by anger, but by pity, and she overflows, not with "every vile deed," but with the good fruits of kindly acts.

without partiality] Here again we have a Greek word which admits of more than one sense. The English version gives it an active sense, as describing the temper which does not distinguish wrongly, which is no respecter of persons. The sense in which the verb, from which the adjective is formed, is used in ch. i. 6, ii. 4, is, however, that of "doubting," or "wavering;" and it seems, therefore, probable that St James means to describe true wisdom as free from the tendency which he thus condemns. That freedom goes naturally with the freedom from unreality which the next word expresses. *Without vacillation* is the condition of "*without hypocrisy.*" Where the purpose is single there is no risk of a simulated piety.

18. *And the fruit of righteousness is sown in peace...*] It is commonly said that "the fruit of righteousness" means "the fruit which is righteousness." The analogy of a like structure, however, in Luke iii. 8 ("worthy fruits of repentance"), Eph. v. 9 ("the fruit of the Spirit"), and other passages, is in favour of taking it as the fruit which righteousness produces. Every good deed is a fruit produced by the good seed sown in the good soil, and not choked by thorns. And every such deed is, in its turn, as the seed of a future fruit like in kind. It is "sown in peace" (we must remember all the fulness of meaning which the Hebrew mind attached to peace as the highest form of blessedness) either "by" or "for" (the former is, perhaps, meant, but the phrase may have been used to include both) those that make peace. We cannot fail to connect these words with the beatitude on the peace-makers in the Sermon on the Mount (Matt. v. 9). We can as little fail to note the resemblance between this portraiture of the true wisdom and the picture which St Paul draws in 1 Cor. xiii. of the excellence of Charity or Love. Differing, as the two teachers did, in many ways, in their modes of thought and language, one fastening on the more practical, the other on the more spiritual, aspects of the Truth, there was an essential agreement in

1—7. *God's giving and the World's getting.*

4 From whence *come* wars and fightings among you? *come they* not hence, *even* of your lusts that war in your mem-
2 bers? Ye lust, and have not: ye kill, and desire *to have*,

their standard of the highest form of the Christian character. A comparison of the two helps us to understand how the one teacher held out the right hand of fellowship to the other (Gal. ii. 9), and to hope for a like accord now among men who seem to differ in their conception of Christian Truth, if only they agree in their ultimate aim and standard, and feel, in the depth of their being, that Love is Wisdom, and that Wisdom is Love.

CH. IV. 1—7. GOD'S GIVING AND THE WORLD'S GETTING.

1. *whence come wars and fightings among you?*...] One source of discord had been touched in the "Be not many masters" of Chap. iii. 1. Sectarianism and all its kindred evils were destructive of peace, and therefore of all true wisdom. Another besetting sin of the race which St James addressed, from which indeed no race or nation is exempt, now comes in view. "Wars," protracted or wide-spread disputes: "fighting," the conflicts and skirmishes of daily life, which make up the campaign,—"What do they come from?" the writer asks, and then makes answer to himself. A question so like in form to this as to suggest the thought that it must be a conscious reproduction, is found in the Epistle of Clement of Rome (c. 45).

even of your lusts that war in your members?] Literally, **from your pleasures.** The noun is used as nearly equivalent to "desires." Common as the word "pleasure" was in all Greek ethical writers, it is comparatively rare in the New Testament. In the Gospels it meets us in Luke viii. 14, and with much the same sense as in this passage. These "lusts" or "pleasures" are, the next word tells us, the hosts that carry on the conflict and perpetuate the warfare. They make our "members," each organ of sense or action, their camping ground and field of battle. Hence, to extend the metaphor one step further, as St Peter extends it, they "war against the soul" (1 Pet. ii. 11).

2. *Ye lust, and have not*...] The *genesis* of evil is traced somewhat in the same way as in ch. i. 15. The germ is found in desire for what we have not, as e. g. in the sins of David (2 Sam. xi. 1) and Ahab (1 Kings xxi. 2—4). That desire becomes the master-passion of a man's soul, and hurries him on to crimes from which he would, at first, have shrunk.

ye kill, and desire to have...] The order strikes us as inverted, putting the last and deadliest sin at the beginning. The marginal alternative of "envy" would doubtless give an easier sense, but this cannot possibly be the meaning of the Greek word as it stands, and comes from a conjectural reading, suggested, without any MS. authority, by Erasmus and Beza. If we remember, however, the state of Jewish society, the bands of robber-outlaws of whom Barabbas was a type (Mark xv. 7;

and cannot obtain: ye fight and war, yet ye have not, because ye ask not. Ye ask, and receive not, because ye ask 3 amiss, that ye may consume *it* upon your lusts. Ye adul- 4 terers and adulteresses, know ye not that the friendship of

John xviii. 39), the "four thousand men that were murderers" of Acts xxi. 38, the bands of Zealots and Sicarii who were prominent in the tumults that preceded the final war with Rome, it will not seem so startling that St James should emphasise his warning by *beginning* with the words "*Ye murder.*" In such a state of society, murder is often the first thing that a man thinks of as a means to gratify his desires, not, as with us, a last resource when other means have failed. Comp. the picture of a like social condition in which "men make haste to shed blood" in Prov. i. 16. There was, perhaps, a grim truth in the picture which St James draws. It was after the deed was done that the murderers began to quarrel over the division of the spoil, and found themselves as unsatisfied as before, still not able to obtain that on which they had set their hearts, and so plunging into fresh quarrels, ending as they began, in bloodshed. There seems, at first, something almost incredible in the thought, that the believers to whom St James wrote could be guilty of such crimes, but Jewish society was at that time rife with atrocities of like nature, and men, nominally disciples of Christ, might then, as in later times, sink to its level. See note on next verse.

ye have not, because ye ask not] This then was the secret of the restless cravings and the ever-returning disappointments. They had never once made their wants the subject of a true and earnest prayer. Here again we note the fundamental unity of teaching in St James and St Paul. Comp. Phil. iv. 6. Prayer is with each of them the condition of content or joy.

3. *Ye ask, and receive not...*] The words are obviously written as in answer to an implied objection: "Not ask," a man might say; "come and listen to our prayers; no one can accuse us of neglecting our devotions." Incredible as it might seem that men plundering and murdering, as the previous verses represent them, should have held such language, or been in any sense, men who prayed, the history of Christendom presents but too many instances of like anomalies. Cornish wreckers going from church to their accursed work, Italian brigands propitiating their patron Saint before attacking a company of travellers, slave-traders, such as John Newton once was, recording piously God's blessing on their traffic of the year;—these may serve to shew how soon conscience may be seared, and its warning voice come to give but an uncertain sound.

that ye may consume it upon your lusts] Better, **that ye may spend it in your pleasures.** This then was that which vitiated all their prayers. They prayed not for the good of others, nor even for their own true good, but for the satisfaction of that which was basest in their nature, and which they, as disciples of Christ, were specially called on to repress.

4. *Ye adulterers and adulteresses...*] The better MSS. give **ye adulteresses** only. The use of the feminine alone in this connexion,

the world is enmity with God? whosoever therefore will be a friend of the world is the enemy of God. Do ye think that the scripture saith in vain, the spirit that dwelleth in us

where the persons referred to are primarily men, is at first startling. It has a partial parallel in our Lord's words "*an evil and adulterous generation*" (Matt. xii. 39), but it finds its best explanation in the thought, not without its bearing on what follows, that the soul's unfaithfulness towards God is like that of a wife towards her husband. It is as though St James said "*Ye adulterous souls.*" There is, it may be, in the use of such a term, a touch of indignant scorn not unlike that in Homer, 'Αχαιΐδες, οὔκετ' 'Αχαιοί. "Women, not men of Achæa" (*Il.* II. 235), or Virgil's "O vere Phrygiæ, neque enim Phryges" (*Æn.* IX. 617). In this subserviency to pleasures, St James sees that which, though united with crimes of violence, is yet essentially effeminate.

the friendship of the world is enmity with God?] Once more we have a distinct echo from the Sermon of the Mount (Matt. vi. 24; Luke xvi. 13). Here, also, as in chap. i. 8, stress is laid on the fact that the neutrality of a divided allegiance is impossible. In that warfare, therefore, we must choose our side. We take it, even if we think that we do not choose it.

whosoever therefore will be a friend of the world...] Literally, **Whosoever wishes to be a friend.** The inference is not a mere repetition, but lays stress on the fact that the mere wish and inclination to be on one side involves, *ipso facto*, antagonism to the other.

5. *the spirit that dwelleth in us lusteth to envy?*] The words present a two-fold difficulty: (1) They are quoted as Scripture, and yet no such words are found either in the Canonical or even in the Apocryphal Books of the Old Testament. (2) It is by no means clear what they mean in themselves, or what is their relation to the context. If we can determine the latter point, it may, perhaps, help us in dealing with the former. (*a*) The better MSS., it may be noted, to begin with, give a different reading of the first words: **The Spirit which he planted** (or **made to dwell) in us.** If we adopt this reading, it makes it all but absolutely certain that what is predicated of the Spirit must be good, and not, as the English version suggests, evil. (*b*) The Greek word for "lusteth" conveys commonly a higher meaning than the English, and is rendered elsewhere by "longing after" (Rom. i. 11; Phil. i. 8, ii. 26; 2 Cor. ix. 14), or "earnestly desiring" (2 Cor. v. 2), or "greatly desiring" (2 Tim. i. 4). New Testament usage is accordingly in favour of giving the word such a meaning here. The verb has no object, but it is natural to supply the pronoun "us." Taking these *data* we get as the true meaning of the words, **The Spirit which He implanted yearns tenderly over us.** (*c*) The words that remain, "to envy," admit of being taken as with an adverbial force. "In a manner tending to envy," **enviously.** The fact that "envy" is elsewhere in the New Testament and elsewhere condemned as simply evil, makes its use here somewhat startling. But the thought implied is that the strongest human affection shews itself in a jealousy which is scarcely distinguishable from "envy." We grudge

lusteth to envy? But he giveth more grace. Wherefore *he* 6
saith, God resisteth the proud, but giveth grace

the transfer to another of the affection which we claim as ours. We *envy* the happiness of that other. In that sense St James says that the Spirit, implanted in us, yearns to make us wholly His and is satisfied with no divided allegiance. He simply treats the Greek word for "envy" as other writers treated the word "jealousy," which though commonly viewed as evil, was yet treated at times as a parable of the purest spiritual affection (2 Cor. xi. 2; Gal. iv. 17, 18). The root-idea of the passage is accordingly identical with that of the jealousy of God over Israel as His bride (Jer. iii. 1—11; Ezek. xvi.: Hos. ii. 3), of His wrath when the bride proved faithless. Those who had been addressed as "adulteresses" (verse 4), were forgetting this. All that they read of the love or jealousy of God was to them as an idle tale. For "in vain" read **idly, emptily.**

There remains the question, in what sense does St James give these words as a quotation from "the Scripture"? No words at all like them in form are found anywhere in the Old Testament, and we have to suppose either (1) that they were cited from some lost book that never found a place in the Hebrew Canon, a supposition, which, though not absolutely impossible, is yet in a very high degree unlikely; or, which seems the more probable explanation, that St James having in his mind the passages above referred to, and many others like them, and finding them too long for quotation, condensed them into one brief pregnant form, which gave the essence of their meaning. A like manner of quoting as Scripture what we do not find in any extant book, is found in Clement of Rome (c. 46), "It has been written, 'Cleave to the saints, for they who cleave to them shall be sanctified.'" As points of detail it may be noted (1) that the Greek word for "yearning" or "longing" occurs in the LXX. version of Deut. xxxii. 11, and is followed in verses 13—19 by an account of the manner in which the love so shewn had been turned to jealousy by the sins of Israel; and (2) that Gen. vi. 5, as in the LXX., "My spirit shall not abide for ever with men," may have suggested the "indwelling" of which the first member of the sentence speaks.

I have given, what seems on the whole, the most tenable explanation of a passage which is admitted on all hands to be one of extreme difficulty. It does not seem desirable to discuss other interpretations at any length, but two or three may be very briefly noticed. (1) The words have been rendered "The Spirit (i.e. the Holy Spirit) that dwelleth in us lusteth against envy," the contrast being assumed to be parallel to that between the works of the Spirit and those of the flesh in Gal. v. 17. There is no sufficient authority, however, for giving this meaning to the preposition. (2) The "spirit" has been referred to man's corrupt will, as "lusting to envy," in its bad sense, but the description of the Spirit as "implanted" or "dwelling" in us, is against this view. (3) In concurrence with the last interpretation, the question "Do ye think that the Scripture speaks in vain?" has been referred to what precedes the statement, that the friendship of the world is enmity with

7 unto the humble. Submit yourselves therefore to God. Resist the devil, and he will flee from you.

8—10. *The Call to Repentance.*

8 Draw nigh to God, and he will draw nigh to you. Cleanse *your* hands, *ye* sinners; and purify *your* hearts, *ye* double

God; but this is at variance with the usual way in which quotations from the Old Testament are introduced in the New.

6. *But he giveth more grace*] Following the explanation already given, the sequence of thought seems to run thus: God loves us with a feeling analogous to the strongest form of jealousy, or even envy, but that jealousy does not lead Him, as it leads men, to be grudging in His gifts; rather does He bestow, as its result, a greater measure of His grace than before, or than He would do, were His attitude towards us one of strict unimpassioned Justice.

Wherefore he saith...] The nominative to the verb is not expressed, and we may, with almost equal fitness, supply the Scripture, the Spirit, or God.

God resisteth the proud, but giveth grace unto the humble] The point of the quotation lies in the last clause, as containing the proof of what St James had just asserted, that God gave His grace freely to those who thought themselves least worthy of it. It is to be noticed (1) that we again find St James quoting from one of the great sapiential books of the Old Testament (Prov. iii. 34), and (2) that St Peter also quotes it (1 Pet. v. 5). That maxim of the wise of old had become, as it were, a law of life for the Community at Jerusalem. Clement of Rome follows their example (c. 30).

7. *Submit yourselves therefore to God*] The forms of the Greek verbs express a somewhat sharper antithesis than the English. God **setteth himself** against the proud, therefore, **set yourselves as under** God.

Resist the devil, and he will flee from you] The rule seems to point to the true field for the exercise of the combative element which enters into man's nature. Not in strife and bitterness against each other, not in setting themselves against the will of God, but in taking their stand against the Enemy of God and man were the disciples of Christ to shew that they were indeed men. We may, perhaps, trace in the form of the precept an indirect reference to the history of the Temptation in Matt. iv. 1—11.

8—10. THE CALL TO REPENTANCE.

8. *Draw nigh to God, and he will draw nigh to you*] The "nearness to God," to which the promise is attached, is primarily that which is involved in all true and earnest prayer, but it should not be forgotten that it includes also the approximation of character and life. We are to walk with God as Enoch walked (Gen. v. 24). The former sense is prominent in the LXX. use of the verb employed by St James, as in Hos. xii. 6, where in the English we have "*wait on* thy God con-

minded. Be afflicted, and mourn, and weep: let your **9** laughter be turned to mourning, and *your* joy to heaviness. Humble yourselves in the sight of the Lord, and he shall lift **10** you up.

11—12. *Rebuke of Evil-speaking.*

Speak not evil one of another, brethren. He that speaketh **11** evil of *his* brother, and judgeth his brother, speaketh evil of

tinually," and Ps. cxix. 169. An illustration of its meaning in the second clause is found in Job xix. 21, where it answers to the English "have pity on me."

Cleanse your hands, ye sinners...] The words contrast, with an implied reference to our Lord's teaching in Matt. xv. 1—9, the true cleanness of hands, which consists in abstinence from the evil that defiles (Ps. xxiv. 4; 1 Tim. ii. 8), with the merely ceremonial cleanness on which the Pharisees laid stress. Comp. Ch. i. 27.

purify your hearts...] The verb implies the same kind of purity as the adjective used in Ch. iii. 17, primarily, that is, *chastity* of heart and life. It has here a special emphasis as contrasted with the "adulteresses" in verse 4, and with the special aspect of the "double-mindedness" which that word implied. See note on Ch. i. 8.

9. *Be afflicted, and mourn, and weep...*] The words are nearly synonymous, the first pointing to the sense of misery (as in "O *wretched* man that I am" in Rom. vii. 24), the second to its general effect on demeanour, the last to its special outflow in tears. The two last verbs are frequently joined together, as in Mark xvi. 10; Luke vi. 25; Rev. xviii. 15. The words are an emphatic call to repentance, and the blessedness which follows on repentance. Here, as so often in the Epistle, we trace the direct influence of the teaching of the Sermon on the Mount (Matt. v. 4). The contrast between the "laughter" and the "mourning" in the clause that follows, makes the connexion all but absolutely certain. The "laughter" is that of the careless, selfish, luxurious rejoicing of the world, the "sport" of the fool in Prov. x. 23.

your joy to heaviness] The Greek for the latter word expresses literally the downcast look of sorrow, and is as old in this sense as Homer,

"Joy to thy foes, but *heavy shame* to thee."
Iliad III. 51.

It exactly describes the attitude of the publican, who would not "lift up so much as his eyes unto heaven" (Luke xviii. 13).

10. *Humble yourselves in the sight of the Lord, and he shall lift you up*] Better, **he shall exalt**, so as to preserve the manifest allusion to our Lord's words as recorded in Matt. xxiii. 12; Luke xiv. 12, xviii. 14. Here again we have another striking parallel with St Peter's language (1 Pet. v. 6). There is, however, a difference as well as an agreement to be noticed. While the other passages speak mainly of humility in its relation to man, this dwells emphatically on its being manifested in relation to God.

the law, and judgeth the law: but if thou judge the law, 12 thou art not a doer of the law, but a judge. There is one lawgiver, who is able to save and to destroy: who art thou that judgest another?

13—17. *Man proposing, God disposing.*

13 Go to now, ye that say, To day or to morrow we will go into such a city, and continue there a year, and buy and sell, and

11, 12. REBUKE OF EVIL-SPEAKING.

11. *Speak not evil one of another, brethren*] The last word indicates the commencement of a new section. It scarcely, however, introduces a new topic. The writer dwells with an iteration, needful for others, and not grievous to himself, (Phil. iii. 1) on the ever-besetting sin of his time and people, against which he had warned his readers in Ch. i. 19, 20, 26, and throughout Ch. iii.

speaketh evil of the law, and judgeth the law...] The logical train of thought seems to run thus. To speak against a brother is to condemn him; to condemn, when no duty calls us to it, is to usurp the function of a judge. One who so usurps becomes *ipso facto* a transgressor of the law, the royal law, of Christ, which forbids judging (Matt. vii. 1—5). The "brother" who is judged is not necessarily such as a member of the Christian society. The superscription of the Epistle includes under that title every one of the family of Abraham, perhaps, every child of Adam.

12. *There is one lawgiver, who is able to save and to destroy...*] Here again we have to trace a latent sequence of thought. The Giver of the Law is, St James implies, the only true and ultimate Judge (comp. 1 Cor. iv. 4, 5), able to award in perfect equity the sentence of salvation or destruction. Men who are called by His appointment to exercise the office of a judge do so as His delegates. Those who are not so called do well to abstain altogether from the work of judging. The description of God as "able to destroy" presents a striking parallel to Matt. x. 28; the question "Who art thou that judgest another?" to Rom. xiv. 4. On this point at least St Paul and St James were of one heart and mind. The word "destroy" does not necessarily either include or exclude the idea of annihilation.

13—17. MAN PROPOSING, GOD DISPOSING.

13. *Go to now, ye that say...*] The warnings pass on to another form of the worldliness of the double-minded; the far-reaching plans for the future such as our Lord had condemned in the parable of the Rich Fool (Luke xii. 16). It is significant that that parable follows in close sequence upon our Lord's disclaimer of the office of a Judge. The opening formula, "Go to," which meets us again in ch. v. 1, is peculiar to St James in the New Testament. It appears in the LXX. in Judg. xix. 6; 2 Kings iv. 24. It is obvious that the warning is

get gain: whereas ye know not what *shall be* on the morrow: 14
for what *is* your life? It is even a vapour, that appeareth
for a little *time*, and then vanisheth away. For that ye *ought* 15
to say, If the Lord will, we shall live, and do this, or that.

addressed to Christians as well as Jews, so far as they were infected by the taint of worldliness. The MSS. vary between "to-day *or* to-morrow" and "to-day *and* to-morrow," the latter implying the contemplation of a two days' journey.

into such a city] Literally, **into this city**, that which was present to the mind of the speaker.

14. *Whereas ye know not what shall be on the morrow*] Literally, **the thing**, or **the event of to-morrow**, the phrase being parallel to "the things of the morrow" in Matt. vi. 34. St James partly reproduces that teaching, partly that of Prov. xxvii. 1.

what is your life?...] Literally, **of what nature** *your life is*. The comparison that follows was one familiar to all the wise of heart who had meditated on the littleness of man's life. It meets us in Job vii. 7; Ps. cii. 3. A yet more striking parallel is found in Wisd. v. 9—14, with which St James may well have been familiar. The word for "vanishing away" occurs, it may be noted, in Wisd. iii. 16. It is not without interest to note at once the agreement and the difference between St James' counsel and that of the popular Epicureanism.

"Quid sit futurum cras, fuge quærere ; et
Quem Fors dierum cumque dabit, lucro
Appone."   HORACE. *Od.* I. 9.

"Strive not the morrow's chance to know,
And count whate'er the Fates bestow,
As given thee for thy gain."

It was not strange that those who thought only of this littleness, should deem that their only wisdom lay in making the most of that little in and by itself, and take "Let us eat and drink, for to-morrow we die" (1 Cor. xv. 32) as their law of life. St James had been taught to connect man's life with a Will higher than his own, and so to take the measure of its greatness as well as of its littleness.

15. *For that ye ought to say...*] Literally, **Instead of saying**, but the English may be admitted as a fair paraphrase.

If the Lord will, we shall live...] This is the reading of the better MSS. The Received Text gives "If the Lord will, and we live, we will do this or that." The sense is substantially the same with either, but it is perhaps, more expressive to refer both life and action to the one Supreme Will. It is better here to refer the word "Lord" to God in His Absolute Unity, without any thought of the distinction of the Persons. The reference of all the contingencies of the future to one supremely wise and loving Will has been in all ages of Christendom the stay and strength of devout souls. It has left its mark, even where it has not always been received as a reality, in familiar formulæ, such as

16 But now ye rejoice in your boastings: all such rejoicing is
17 evil. Therefore to him that knoweth to do good, and doeth
it not, to him it is sin.

1—6. *Warnings for the Rich.*

5 Go to now, ye rich *men*, weep and howl for your
2 miseries that shall come upon *you*. Your riches are cor-

"God willing," *Deo Volente*, or even the abbreviated D. V. There
is, perhaps, a special interest in noting that St Paul uses the self-same
formula as St James in reference to his plans for the future (1 Cor.
iv. 19).

16. *But now ye rejoice in your boastings*] Better, **ye exult in your
vain glories.** If the words were not too familiar, **ye glory in your
braggings** would, perhaps, be a still nearer equivalent. The noun
is found in 1 John ii. 16 ("the *pride* of life"), and not elsewhere in
the New Testament. It is defined by Aristotle (*Eth. Nicom.* IV. 13)
as the character of the man who lays claim to what will bring him credit
when the claim is either altogether false or grossly exaggerated. He
contrasts it with the "irony" which deliberately, with good or bad
motive, understates its claims. The "now" is more or less emphatic,
= "as things are."

17. *Therefore to him that knoweth to do good...*] The law of
conscience is here enforced in its utmost width. To leave undone
what we know we ought to do, is sin, even though there be no outward
act of what men call crime or vice. The bearing of the general axiom
on the immediate context is obviously that though men assented then,
as we too often assent, to the abstract truth of the shortness of life and
the uncertainty of the future, they went on practically as before with
far-stretching calculations. Such men need to be reminded that this
inconsistency is of the very essence of sin.

CH. V. 1—6. WARNINGS FOR THE RICH.

1. *Go to now, ye rich men, weep and howl*] The words are nearly
the same as those we have met with before in ch. iv. 9, but there is
in them less of the call to repentance, and more of the ring of prophetic
denunciation. The word for "howl," not found elsewhere in the
New Testament, is found in three consecutive chapters of Isaiah (xiii.
6, xiv. 31, xv. 3), which may well have been present to St James'
thoughts.

for your miseries that shall come upon you] Literally, **that are coming
upon you,** in the very act to come. The context points to these as
consisting not merely in the cares and anxieties that come in the
common course of things upon the rich, but in the special troubles
that were to usher in the advent of the Judge. Historically, the words
had their primary fulfilment in the woes that preceded the destruction
of Jerusalem, but these were but the first in the series of "springing

rupted, and your garments are motheaten. Your gold and 3 silver is cankered; and the rust of them shall be a witness against you, and shall eat your flesh as *it were* fire : ye have heaped treasure together for the last days. Behold, the hire 4 of the labourers which have reaped *down* your fields, which

and germinant accomplishments" which will attain their completeness before the final Advent.

2. *Your riches are corrupted, and your garments are motheaten*] The union of the two chief forms of Eastern wealth in this and the following verse, reminds us of the like combination in Matt. vi. 19, "where moth and rust doth corrupt." Comp. St Paul's "I have coveted no man's silver, or gold, or apparel" (Acts xx. 33).

3. *Your gold and silver is cankered*] Literally, **rusted,** the word being used generically of the tarnish that sooner or later comes over all metals that are exposed to the action of the air.

shall be a witness against you...] Better, **for a witness to you.** The doom that falls on the earthly possessions of the ungodly shall be, as it were, the token of what will fall on them, unless they avert it by repentance.

shall eat your flesh as it were fire] The last words have been sometimes taken as belonging to the next clause, "as fire ye laid up treasure," but the structure of the English text is preferable. The underlying image suggested is that the rust or canker spreads from the riches to the very life itself, and that when they fail, and leave behind them only the sense of wasted opportunities and the memories of evil pleasures, the soul will shudder at their work as the flesh shudders at the touch of fire. We may perhaps trace a reminiscence of the "unquenchable fire" devouring the carcases in Gehenna, as in Mark ix. 44.

Ye have heaped treasure together for the last days] Better, **Ye laid** (or, *ye have laid*) **up treasure in the last days.** The preposition cannot possibly have the sense of "for." St James shared the belief of other New Testament writers that they were living in "the last days" of the world's history, and that the "coming of the Lord" was nigh (1 John ii. 18; 1 Cor. xv. 51; 1 Thess. iv. 15). For those to whom he wrote the words had a very real truth. They were actually living in the "last days" of the polity of Israel. In the chaos and desolation of its fall their heaped-up treasures would avail but little. They would be marked out in proportion to their wealth, as the first to be attacked and plundered.

4. *Behold, the hire of the labourers*...] The evil was one of old standing in Judæa. The law had condemned those who kept back the wages of the hired labourer even for a single night (Lev. xix. 13). Jeremiah (xxii. 13) had uttered a woe against him "that useth his neighbour's service without wages." Malachi (iii. 5) had spoken of the swift judgment that should come on those who "oppressed the hireling in his wages." The grasping avarice that characterized the latter days of Judaism shewed itself in this form of oppression among others.

is of you kept back by fraud, crieth: and the cries of them which have reaped are entered into the ears of the Lord of ⁵ sabaoth. Ye have lived in pleasure on the earth, and been wanton; ye have nourished your hearts, as in a day of ⁶ slaughter. Ye have condemned *and* killed the just; *and* he doth not resist you.

are entered into the ears of the Lord of sabaoth] The divine Name thus used was pre-eminently characteristic of the language of the Prophets. It does not appear at all in the Pentateuch, nor in Joshua, Judges, or Ruth; and probably took its rise in the Schools of the Prophets, founded by Samuel. Whether its primary meaning was that Jehovah was the God of all the armies of earth, the God, as we say, of battles, or that He ruled over the armies of the stars of heaven, or over the unseen hosts of angels, or was wide enough, as seems probable, to include all three ideas, is a question which cannot be very definitely answered. It is characteristic of St James that he gives the Hebrew form of the word, as also St Paul does in citing Isai. i. 9 in Rom. ix. 29. For the most part the LXX. renders it by "Almighty" (*Pantokratōr*), and in this form it appears in Rev. iv. 8, where "Holy, holy, holy, Lord God Almighty" answers to " Lord God of sabaoth," or "of hosts" in Isai. vi. 3. This title is specially characteristic of Malachi, in whom it occurs not less than 23 times.

5. *Ye have lived in pleasure on the earth, and been wanton*] Better, **Ye lived luxuriously** *and* **spent wantonly**, the latter word emphasising the lavish and profligate expenditure by which the luxury which the former expresses was maintained.

ye have nourished your hearts, as in a day of slaughter] Many of the best MSS. omit the particle of comparison, **ye nourished your heart in the day of slaughter**. With this reading, the "day of slaughter" is that of the carnage and bloodshed of war, such a "sacrifice" as that which the Lord of Hosts had, of old, by the river Euphrates (Jerem. xlvi. 10), or the "great slaughter" in the land of Idumæa (Isai. xxxiv. 6). The "rich men" of Judæa, in their pampered luxury, were but fattening themselves, all unconscious of their doom, as beasts are fattened, for the slaughter. The insertion of the particle of comparison suggests a different aspect of the same thought. A sacrifice was commonly followed by a sumptuous feast upon what had been offered. Comp. the union of the two thoughts in the harlot's words ("I have peace-offerings with me; this day have I paid my vows") in Prov. vii. 14. Taking this view St James reproaches the self-indulgent rich with making their life one long continuous feast. The former interpretation seems preferable, both on critical and exegetical grounds.

6. *Ye have condemned and killed the just*] The words have been very generally understood as referring to the death of Christ, and on this view, the words "he doth not resist you" have been interpreted as meaning, "He no longer checks you in your career of guilt; He leaves you alone (comp. Hos. iv. 17) to fill up the measure of your sin."

7—11. *Comfort and Counsel for the Poor.*

Be patient therefore, brethren, unto the coming of the 7 Lord. Behold, the husbandman waiteth for the precious

St James, it has been inferred, uses the term "the Just One" as Stephen had done (Acts vii. 52), as pointing emphatically to "Jesus Christ the righteous" (1 John ii. 1). Fuller consideration, however, shews that such a meaning could hardly have come within the horizon of St James's thoughts. (1) That single evil act of priests, and scribes, and the multitude of Jerusalem, could hardly have been thus spoken of in an Epistle addressed to the Twelve Tribes of the dispersion, without a more distinct indication of what was referred to. To see in them, as some have done, the statement that the Jews, wherever they were found, were guilty of that crime, as accepting and approving it, or as committing sins which made such an atonement necessary, is to read into them a non-natural meaning. (2) The whole context leads us to see in the words, a generic evil, a class sin, characteristic, like those of the previous verse, of the rich and powerful everywhere. (3) The meaning thus given to "he doth not resist you" seems, to say the least, strained and unnatural, especially as coming so soon after the teaching (ch. iv. 6) which had declared that "God does *resist* the proud." (4) The true meaning of both clauses is found, it is believed, in taking "the just" as the representative of a class, probably of the class of those, who as disciples of Christ the Just One, were reproducing His pattern of righteousness. Such an one, like his Master, and like Stephen, St James adds, takes as his law (note the change of tense from past to present) the rule of not resisting. He submits patiently, certain that in the end he will be more than conqueror. It is not without interest to note that that title was afterwards applied to St James himself (Euseb. *Hist.* II. 23). The name Justus, which appears three times in the New Testament (Acts i. 23, xviii. 7; Col. iv. 11), was obviously the Latin equivalent of this epithet, and it probably answered to the *Chasidim* or Assideans (1 Macc. ii. 42, vii. 13, 2 Macc. xiv. 6) of an earlier stage of Jewish religious history. It is as if a follower of George Fox had addressed the judges and clergy of Charles II.'s reign, and said to them, "Ye persecuted *the Friend*, and he does not resist you." (5) It is in favour of this interpretation that it presents a striking parallel to a passage in the "Wisdom of Solomon," with which this Epistle has so many affinities. There too the writer speaks of the wealthy and voluptuous as laying snares for "the just" who is also "poor," who calls himself "the **servant** of the Lord," and boasts of God as his Father (Wisd. ii. 12—16). Comp. also the description of the ultimate triumph of the just man in Wisd. v. 1—5.

7—11. COMFORT AND COUNSEL FOR THE POOR.

7. *Be patient therefore*] More literally, **Be long-suffering**. The logical sequence implied in "therefore" is that the "brethren" whom St James addresses should follow the example of the ideal "just man" of whom the previous verse had spoken. There is a *terminus ad quem*

fruit of the earth, and hath long patience for it, until he 8 receive the early and latter rain. Be ye also patient; stablish your hearts: for the coming of the Lord draweth 9 nigh. Grudge not one against another, brethren, lest ye be condemned: behold, the judge standeth before the 10 door. Take, my brethren, the prophets, who have spoken

for that long-suffering, and it is found in "the coming of the Lord." Here, with scarcely the shadow of a doubt, it is the Lord Jesus who is meant. St James had learned from the discourse recorded in Matt. xxiv. 3, 37, 39, to think of that Advent as redressing the evils of the world, and he shared the belief, natural in that age of the Church, that it was not far off. It had already drawn nigh (verse 8). The patient expectation of the sufferers would not be frustrated. We see that the hope was not fulfilled as men expected, but we may believe that even for those who cherished it, it was not in vain. There was a judgment at hand, in which evil-doers received their just reward, and which made glad the hearts of the righteous.

hath long patience for it] The verb is the same as that just translated "be patient." Better, perhaps, **is long-suffering over it**, as implying a kind of watchful expectancy. The prevalence of a long-continued drought in Palestine when St James wrote (see note on verse 16) gave, we can scarcely doubt, a very special emphasis to his words of counsel.

until he receive the early and latter rain] The MSS. present a singular variety of readings, some giving "rain," some "fruit," and some no substantive at all. "Rain" gives the best meaning. The "early rain" fell in the months from October to February; the latter, from March to the end of April. Comp. Deut. xi. 14; Jer. iii. 3, v. 24; Joel ii. 23. An ingenious allegorising interpretation finds in the "early" rain the tears of youthful repentance; in the "latter," those of age.

8. *Be ye also patient*] Better, **long-suffering**; as before.

stablish your hearts] Better, **strengthen**. The strength is to come from the thought that the great Advent has come near, that there will be a great Court of Appeal from all man's injustice. Here, as before, we note a hope which was not fulfilled as men expected its fulfilment, and yet was not frustrated. The promise of the second Advent has been to believers in Christ what the promise of the first Advent was to Abraham and the patriarchs. They saw the far-off fulfilment, knowing not the times and seasons, and it made them feel that they were strangers and pilgrims (Heb. xi. 13), and so purified and strengthened them.

9. *Grudge not one against another...*] Better, perhaps, **complain not**. The primary meaning of the verb is "to groan." To indulge in such complaints was to assume the office of the Judge, whose presence they ought to think of as not far off, even "at the door," and so brought with it the condemnation which He himself had pronounced (Matt. vii. 1). The standing before the door presents a point of comparison with Rev. iii. 20.

10. *Take, my brethren, the prophets...*] Better, as representing the

in the name of the Lord, for an example of suffering affliction, and of patience. Behold, we count them happy which endure. Ye have heard of the patience of Job, and have seen the end of the Lord; that the Lord is very pitiful, and of tender mercy.

emphatic order of the Greek, **As an example of affliction and long-suffering take, my brethren, the prophets**...... The first of the nouns expresses simply the objective affliction, not the manner of enduring it.

the prophets who have spoken...] Better, **who spake.** The words point, perhaps, chiefly to the prophets of the Old Testament, as having, with scarcely an exception, suffered persecution (Matt. v. 12). But we must not forget that there were prophets also in the Christian Church (1 Cor. xii. 10, xiv. 24, 29; Eph. ii. 20, iv. 11; Rev. xxii. 9), and that these were exposed to the same trials as their predecessors. It is to their sufferings that St Paul probably referred in 1 Thess. ii. 15, and St James may well have included them in his general reference. Stephen and his own namesake, the son of Zebedee, may have been specially present to his thoughts.

11. *we count them happy which endure*...] Better, **we call them blessed**, the verb being formed from the adjective used in ch. i. 12. Comp. Luke ii. 48. The words may contain a reference to Dan. xii. 12.

Ye have heard of the patience of Job] Better, **endurance**, to keep up the connexion with the verb. It is singular that, though the book is once quoted (1 Cor. iii. 19, Job v. 13), this is the only reference in the New Testament to the history of Job. Philo, however, quotes from Job xiv. 4 (*de Mutat. Nom.* XXIV.), and he is referred to by Clement of Rome (1. 17. 26). The book would naturally be studied by one whose attention had been drawn, as St James's manifestly had been, to the sapiential Books included in the Hagiographa of the Old Testament. It is obvious that he refers to the book as containing an actual history, as obvious that his so referring to it throws no light on the questions which have been raised, but which it would be out of place to discuss here, as to its authorship and date.

and have seen the end of the Lord] The words have received two very different interpretations. (1) They have been referred to the "end" which the "Lord" wrought out for Job after his endurance had been tried, as in Job xlii. 12. (2) The "end of the Lord" has been understood as pointing to the death and resurrection of Christ as the Lord who had been named in verse 7, the highest example of patience in the Old Testament being brought into juxtaposition with the Highest of all Examples. On this view the passage becomes parallel with 1 Peter ii. 19—25. The clause that follows is, however, decisively in favour of (1), nor is there any instance of a New Testament writer using the term "end" of the passion and death of Christ. Matt. xxvi. 58, which is the nearest approach to such a use, is scarcely in point.

that the Lord is very pitiful, and of tender mercy] The first of the two adjectives, of which the nearest English equivalent would be **large-hearted** or perhaps **tender-hearted**, is not found in any other writer,

12. *Oaths.*

¹² But above all *things*, my brethren, swear not, neither by heaven, neither by the earth, neither by any other oath: but let your yea be yea; and *your* nay, nay; lest ye fall into condemnation.

13—16. *Affliction—Sickness—Confession.*

¹³ Is any among you afflicted? let him pray. Is any merry?

and may have been a coinage of St James's. The latter occurs in Ecclus. ii. 11, in close juxtaposition with a passage which we have already found referred to in the Epistle (Ecclus. ii. 11), and which may therefore have been present to St James's thoughts. In this instance "the Lord" is clearly used in the Old Testament sense, and this, as has been said, determines the meaning of the previous clause.

12. OATHS.

12. *above all things, my brethren, swear not*...] The passage presents so close a parallel with Matt. v. 33—37 that it is almost a necessary inference that St James, if not himself a hearer of the Sermon on the Mount, had become acquainted with it as reported by others. Comp. *Introduction*, p. 8. The words condemn alike the rash use of oaths in common speech, and the subtle distinctions drawn by the Scribes as to the binding force of this or that formula (Matt. xxiii. 16—22). That the condemnation does not extend to the solemn judicial use of oaths we see in the facts (1) that our Lord answered when questioned as on oath by Caiaphas (Matt. xxvi. 63, 64), and (2) that St Paul at times used modes of expression which are essentially of the nature of an oath (2 Cor. i. 23; Romans i. 9; Gal. i. 20; Phil. i. 8). It is not without interest to note that in this respect also the practice of the Essenes, in their efforts after holiness, was after the pattern of the teaching of St James. They, too, avoided oaths as being no less an evil than perjury itself (Joseph. *Wars*. II. 8. 85). They, however, with a somewhat strange inconsistency, bound the members of their own society by "tremendous oaths" of obedience and secresy.

13—16. AFFLICTION—SICKNESS—CONFESSION.

13. *Is any among you afflicted, let him pray*...] The precepts point to the principle that worship is the truest and best expression of both sorrow and joy. In affliction men are not to groan or complain against others, or murmur against God, but to pray for help and strength and wisdom. When they are "merry" (better, **of good cheer**) they are not to indulge in riotous or boastful mirth, but to "sing psalms." The verb is used by St Paul (Rom. xv. 9; 1 Cor. xiv. 15; Eph. v. 19). Primarily it was used of instrumental string music, but, as in the word "Psalm," had been transferred to the words of which that music was the natural accompaniment. It is, perhaps, specially characteristic

let him sing psalms. Is any sick among you? let him call 14
for the elders of the church; and let them pray over him,
anointing him with oil in the name of the Lord: and the 15

of St James that he contemplates what we may call the individual
use of such music as well as the congregational, as a help to the spiritual
life. We are reminded of two memorable instances of this employment
in the lives of George Herbert and Milton. Compare also Hooker's
grand words on the power of Psalmody and Music (*Eccl. Pol.* v. 38).

14. *Is any sick among you? let him call for the elders of the church*] The
rule is full of meaning. (1) As regards the functions of the Elders of the
Church. Over and above special gifts of prophecy or teaching, they
were to visit the sick, not merely for spiritual comfort and counsel, but
as possessing "gifts of healing" (1 Cor. xii. 9). (2) The use of the term
"Elders" exactly agrees with the account of the Jewish Church in
Acts xi. 30, xv. 6, xxi. 18. In the Gentile Churches the Greek title of
Bishop (*Episcopos* = overseer) came into use as a synonym for "Elder"
(Acts xx. 28; Phil. i. 1; 1 Tim. iii. 1; Tit. i. 5, 7), but within the limits
of the New Testament the Church of Jerusalem has only "Apostles and
Elders." It may fairly be inferred from the position which he occupies
in Acts xv. that St James himself was reckoned as belonging to the first
of the two classes. St Paul's way of mentioning him naturally, though
not necessarily, implies the same fact (Gal. i. 19).

anointing him with oil in the name of the Lord] The context shews
that this was done as a means of healing. It had been the practice of
the Twelve during part, at least, of our Lord's ministry (Mark vi. 13).
The Parable of the good Samaritan gives one example of the medical
use of oil (Luke x. 34), another is found in Isai. i. 6. Friction with
olive oil was prescribed by Celsus for fever. Herod the Great used oil-
baths (Joseph. *Ant.* XVII. 6. § 5). The principle implied in the use of
oil instead of the direct exercise of supernatural gifts without any medium
at all, was probably, in part, analogous to our Lord's employment of
like *media* in the case of the blind and deaf (Mark vii. 33, viii. 23;
John ix. 6). It served as a help to the faith of the person healed;
perhaps also, in the case of the Apostles, to that of the healer. The
position of the disciples was not that of men trusting in charms or
spells and boasting of their powers, but rather that of those who used
simple natural means of healing in dependence on God's blessing. A
sanction was implicitly given to the use of all outward means as not
inconsistent with faith in the power of prayer, to the prayer of faith as
not excluding the use of any natural means. "The Lord" in whose Name
this was to be done is here, without doubt, definitely the Lord Jesus.
Comp. Matt. xviii. 5; Mark ix. 39; Luke ix. 49; Acts iii. 16, iv. 10, 18,
30. The subsequent history of the practice is not without interest. It
does not seem to have been ever entirely dropped either in the West or
East. In the latter, though miraculous gifts of healing no longer
accompanied it, it was, and still is, employed ostensibly as a means of
healing, and the term "*extreme* unction" has been carefully rejected.
Stress is laid on the words of St James as pointing to the collective

prayer of faith shall save the sick, and the Lord shall raise him up; and if he have committed sins, they shall be for-

action of the elders, not to that of a single elder, and the legitimate number ranges from three as a minimum to seven. It is evident that here the idea of united prayer working with natural means has, in theory at least, survived. In the West, on the other hand, a new theory grew up with the growth of Scholasticism. If bodily healing no longer followed, it was because the anointing had become the sign and sacrament of a spiritual healing, and the special grace which it conveyed was thought of as being specifically different from that which came through other channels, adapted to the needs of the soul in its last struggles. So the term "Extreme Unction" came into use in the twelfth century, and the Council of Trent (*Catech*. VI. 2. 9) limited its use to those who were manifestly drawing near unto death, and gave it the title of "*sacramentum exeuntium*." In the First Prayer Book of Edward VI. the rite was retained, partly, it would seem, by way of compromise ("if the sick person desire to be anointed"), partly, as the language of the prayer that was to accompany the act seems to indicate (" our heavenly Father vouchsafe for His great mercy (if it be His blessed will) to restore to thee thy bodily health"), with a faint hope of reviving the original idea. In the Prayer Book of 1552, the "unction" disappeared, and has never since been revived.

15. *and the prayer of faith shall save the sick*] The context leaves no doubt that the primary thought is, as in our Lord's words to men and women whom He healed, "Thy faith hath saved thee"—"thy faith hath made thee whole" (Matt. ix. 22; Mark v. 34, x. 52; Luke vii. 50, viii. 48, xvii. 19, xviii. 42), that the sick man should in such a case "recover his bodily health." The "prayer of faith" was indeed not limited to that recovery in its scope, but the answer to that prayer in its higher aims, is given separately afterwards in the promise of forgiveness.

and the Lord shall raise him up] Here, as in verse 14, we have to think of St James as recognising not merely the power of God generally, but specifically that of the Lord Jesus, still working through His servants, as He worked personally on earth. So Peter said to Æneas, "Jesus Christ maketh thee whole" (Acts ix. 34).

if he have committed sins...] The Greek expresses with a subtle distinction, hard to reproduce in English, the man's being in the state produced by having committed sins. Repentance, it is obvious, is presupposed as a condition, and the love of God in Christ as the fountain of forgiveness, but the prayer of the elders of the Church is, beyond question, represented as instrumental, as helping to win for the sinner the grace both of repentance and forgiveness. It is noticeable that the remission of sins thus promised is dependent not on the utterance of the quasi-judicial formula of the *Absolvo te* (that, indeed, was not used at all until the 13th century) by an individual priest, but on the prayer of the elders as representing the Church. Comp. John xx. 23, where also the promise is in the plural, " Whosesoever sins *ye* remit."

given him. Confess *your* faults one to another, and pray one for another, that ye may be healed.

16—20. *Prayer and Conversion.*

The effectual fervent prayer of a righteous *man* availeth much. Elias was a man subject to like passions as we are,

16. *Confess your faults one to another*...] Better, with the old MSS. **Therefore** *confess*—and **transgressions** instead of *faults*. The noun includes sins against God as well as against men : the words refer the rule of this mutual confession to the promise of forgiveness as its ground. In details the precept is singularly wide. The confession is not to be made by the layman to the elder, more than by the elder to the layman. In either case the question whether it was to be public or private, spontaneous or carried on by questions, is left open. Examples such as those of Matt. iii. 6; Acts xix. 18, 19, suggest the thought of the public confession of individual sins, which was, indeed, the practice of the Church of the third and fourth centuries, as it was afterwards that of many Monastic orders. A later revival of the custom is found in the "class-meetings" of the followers of John Wesley. The closing words, *that ye may be healed*, have been thought to limit the counsel thus given to times of sickness. It may be admitted that the words are to be taken primarily of bodily healing, but on the other hand, the tense of the imperatives implies continuous action. The writer urges the habit of mutual prayer and intercession, that when sickness comes, there may be a quicker work of healing in the absence of spiritual impediments to the exercise of supernatural powers working through natural *media*.

16—20. PRAYER AND CONVERSION.

The effectual fervent prayer of a righteous man availeth much] The words "effectual fervent" represent a single participle (*energumenè*), which is commonly rendered (as in 2 Cor. i. 6; Gal. v. 6; 1 Thess. ii. 13) by "working." That accordingly may be its meaning here: *A righteous man's supplication is of great might in its working.* The later ecclesiastical use of the word, however, suggests another explanation. The *Energumeni* were those who were acted, or worked, on by an evil spirit, and the word became a synonym for the "demoniacs" of the New Testament. It is possible that a like passive meaning may be intended here, and that the participle describes the character of a prayer which is more than the utterance of mere human feeling, in which the Spirit itself is making intercession with us (Rom. viii. 26).

17. *Elias was a man subject to like passions as we are*] The word is the same as that used by St Paul in Acts xiv. 15. The reference to the history of Elijah (1 Kings xvii. 1, xviii. 1) is noticeable, as one of the coincidences on which stress has been laid as suggesting the inference that the Epistle was written by the son of Zebedee, whose thoughts had been directed to the history of Elijah by the Transfiguration, and who and he prayed earnestly that it might not rain: and it rained not on the earth *by the space of* three years and six 18 months. And he prayed again, and the heaven gave rain, and the earth brought forth her fruit.

19 Brethren, if any of you do err from the truth, and one 20 convert him; let him know, that he which converteth the

had himself referred to that history when he sought to call down fire from heaven on the village of the Samaritans (Luke ix. 54). The inference is, at the best, uncertain. It is, perhaps, more to the purpose to note that the son of Sirach, with whose teaching that of the Epistle presents so many parallels, had dwelt with great fulness on the history of Elijah (Ecclus. xlviii. 1—12). It is remarkable that the Old Testament narrative does not directly state that the drought and the rain came as an answer to Elijah's prayer, and that this is therefore an inference drawn by St James from the fact of the attitude of supplication described in 1 Kings xviii. 42. An interesting coincidence in connexion with this reference to Elijah's history presents itself in the narrative given in Josephus (*Ant.* XVIII. 8, § 6) of the troubles caused by Caligula's insane attempt to set up his statue in the Temple at Jerusalem. Petronius, the then Governor of Judæa, was moved by the passionate entreaties of the people, and supported the efforts made by Agrippa I., who remained at Rome, to turn the Emperor from his purpose. It was one of the years of drought that brought about the great famine foretold by Agabus (Acts xi. 28). No rain had fallen for many weeks, and the people—Christians, we may well believe, as well as Jews, though Josephus, of course, makes no mention of the former—were "instant in prayer," calling upon the Lord God of Israel to send rain upon the earth. Suddenly rain fell in a plenteous shower from an almost cloudless sky. The earth was refreshed, and the pressing danger averted. Petronius, Josephus relates, was much moved by this manifestation, this *Epiphany*, of the Divine Power, and looked upon it partly as an answer to the prayers of the people, partly as the reward of the equity which he had shewn in dealing with them. According to the date which, on independent grounds, has here been assigned to St James's Epistle, the event referred to must have happened but a few months before, or but a few months after, it. If before, he may well have had it in his thoughts. If after, it may well have been in part the effect of his teaching. Students of Church History will remember the strikingly parallel instance of the prayers of the soldiers of the Thundering Legion in the Expedition of Marcus Aurelius against the Marcomanni (Euseb. *Hist.* v. 5. Tertull. *Apol.* c. 5).

19. *if any of you do err from the truth, and one convert him*...] Better, as the verb is passive, *if any of you* **be led astray.** The "truth" here is obviously not the faith which was common to Jews and Christians, but specifically "the truth as it is in Jesus," the truth which the "brethren," who held the faith of the Lord Jesus Christ" (ch. ii. 1), had received as their inheritance. To convert one who had so strayed, in thought or will, in belief or act, was to bring him back to the truth.

sinner from the error of his way shall save a soul from death, and shall hide a multitude of sins.

20. *from the error of his way*] The noun always involves the idea of being deceived as well as erring. Comp. 2 Pet. ii. 18, iii. 17; 1 John iv. 6.

shall save a soul from death] The soul is obviously that of the sinner who is converted. Death, bodily and spiritual, would be the outcome of the error if he were left alone, and in being rescued from the error he is therefore saved also from death.

and shall hide a multitude of sins] The phrase is one of those which St James has in common with St Peter (1 Pet. iv. 8). It occurs also in the LXX. of Ps. lxxxv. 2, and in a nearly identical form in Ps. xxxii. 1. The Hebrew, and English version, of Prov. x. 12 present a still closer parallel, but the LXX. seems to have followed a different text, and gives "Friendship covers all those that are not contentious." The context leaves hardly any room for doubt that the "sins" which are thought of as covered are primarily those of the man converted, and not those of the converter. There is, however, a studied generality in the form of the teaching, which seems to emphasise the wide blessedness of love. In the very act of seeking to convert one for whom we care we must turn to God ourselves, and in covering the past sins of another our own also are covered. In such an act love reaches its highest point, and that love includes the faith in God which is the condition of forgiveness.

The absence of any formal close to the Epistle is in many ways remarkable. In this respect it stands absolutely alone in the New Testament, the nearest approach to it being found in 1 John v. 21. It is a possible explanation of this peculiarity, that we have lost the conclusion of the Epistle. It is, however, more probable that the abruptness is that of emphasis. The writer had given utterance to a truth which he desired above all things to impress on the minds of his readers, and he could not do this more effectually than by making it the last word he wrote to them.

Cambridge

PRINTED BY C. J. CLAY M.A. AND SONS
AT THE UNIVERSITY PRESS

GENERAL EDITOR, THE VERY REV. J. J. S. PEROWNE,
DEAN OF PETERBOROUGH.

Opinions of the Press.

"*It is difficult to commend too highly this excellent series.*"—Guardian.

"*The modesty of the general title of this series has, we believe, led many to misunderstand its character and underrate its value. The books are well suited for study in the upper forms of our best schools, but not the less are they adapted to the wants of all Bible students who are not specialists. We doubt, indeed, whether any of the numerous popular commentaries recently issued in this country will be found more serviceable for general use.*"—Academy.

"*One of the most popular and useful literary enterprises of the nineteenth century.*"—Baptist Magazine.

"*Of great value. The whole series of comments for schools is highly esteemed by students capable of forming a judgment. The books are scholarly without being pretentious: and information is so given as to be easily understood.*"—Sword and Trowel.

"*The value of the work as an aid to Biblical study, not merely in schools but among people of all classes who are desirous to have intelligent knowledge of the Scriptures, cannot easily be over-estimated.*"—The Scotsman.

The Book of Judges. J. J. LIAS, M.A. "His introduction is clear and concise, full of the information which young students require, and indicating the lines on which the various problems suggested by the Book of Judges may be solved."—*Baptist Magazine.*

1 Samuel, by A. F. KIRKPATRICK. "Remembering the interest with which we read the *Books of the Kingdom* when they were appointed as a subject for school work in our boyhood, we have looked with some eagerness into Mr Kirkpatrick's volume, which contains the first instalment of them. We are struck with the great improvement in character, and variety in the materials, with which schools are now supplied. A clear map inserted in each volume, notes suiting the convenience of the scholar and the difficulty of the passage, and not merely dictated by the fancy of the commentator, were luxuries which a quarter of a century ago the Biblical student could not buy."—*Church Quarterly Review.*

"To the valuable series of Scriptural expositions and elementary commentaries which is being issued at the Cambridge University Press, under the title 'The Cambridge Bible for Schools,' has been added **The First Book of Samuel** by the Rev. A. F. KIRKPATRICK. Like other volumes of the series, it contains a carefully written historical and critical introduction, while the text is profusely illustrated and explained by notes."—*The Scotsman.*

10,000
23/12/90

II. Samuel. A. F. KIRKPATRICK, M.A. "Small as this work is in mere dimensions, it is every way the best on its subject and for its purpose that we know of. The opening sections at once prove the thorough competence of the writer for dealing with questions of criticism in an earnest, faithful and devout spirit; and the appendices discuss a few special difficulties with a full knowledge of the data, and a judicial reserve, which contrast most favourably with the superficial dogmatism which has too often made the exegesis of the Old Testament a field for the play of unlimited paradox and the ostentation of personal infallibility. The notes are always clear and suggestive; never trifling or irrelevant; and they everywhere demonstrate the great difference in value between the work of a commentator who is also a Hebraist, and that of one who has to depend for his Hebrew upon secondhand sources."—*Academy*.

"The Rev. A. F. KIRKPATRICK has now completed his commentary on the two books of Samuel. This second volume, like the first, is furnished with a scholarly and carefully prepared critical and historical introduction, and the notes supply everything necessary to enable the merely English scholar—so far as is possible for one ignorant of the original language—to gather up the precise meaning of the text. Even Hebrew scholars may consult this small volume with profit."—*Scotsman*.

I. Kings and Ephesians. "With great heartiness we commend these most valuable little commentaries. We had rather purchase these than nine out of ten of the big blown up expositions. Quality is far better than quantity, and we have it here."—*Sword and Trowel*.

I. Kings. "This is really admirably well done, and from first to last there is nothing but commendation to give to such honest work."—*Bookseller*.

II. Kings. "The Introduction is scholarly and wholly admirable, while the notes must be of incalculable value to students."—*Glasgow Herald*.

"It is equipped with a valuable introduction and commentary, and makes an admirable text book for Bible-classes."—*Scotsman*.

"It would be difficult to find a commentary better suited for general use."—*Academy*.

The Book of Job. "Able and scholarly as the Introduction is, it is far surpassed by the detailed exegesis of the book. In this Dr DAVIDSON's strength is at its greatest. His linguistic knowledge, his artistic habit, his scientific insight, and his literary power have full scope when he comes to exegesis.... The book is worthy of the reputation of Dr Davidson; it represents the results of many years of labour, and it will greatly help to the right understanding of one of the greatest works in the literature of the world."—*The Spectator*.

"In the course of a long introduction, Dr DAVIDSON has presented us with a very able and very interesting criticism of this wonderful book. Its contents, the nature of its composition, its idea and purpose, its integrity, and its age are all exhaustively treated of.... We have not space to examine fully the text and notes before us, but we can, and do heartily, recommend the book, not only for the upper forms in schools, but to Bible students and teachers generally. As we wrote of a previous volume in the same series, this one leaves nothing to be desired. The notes are full and suggestive, without being too long, and, in itself, the introduction forms a valuable addition to modern Bible literature."—*The Educational Times.*

"Already we have frequently called attention to this exceedingly valuable work as its volumes have successively appeared. But we have never done so with greater pleasure, very seldom with so great pleasure, as we now refer to the last published volume, that on the **Book of Job**, by Dr DAVIDSON, of Edinburgh....We cordially commend the volume to all our readers. The least instructed will understand and enjoy it; and mature scholars will learn from it."—*Methodist Recorder.*

Job—Hosea. " It is difficult to commend too highly this excellent series, the volumes of which are now becoming numerous. The two books before us, small as they are in size, comprise almost everything that the young student can reasonably expect to find in the way of helps towards such general knowledge of their subjects as may be gained without an attempt to grapple with the Hebrew; and even the learned scholar can hardly read without interest and benefit the very able introductory matter which both these commentators have prefixed to their volumes. It is not too much to say that these works have brought within the reach of the ordinary reader resources which were until lately quite unknown for understanding some of the most difficult and obscure portions of Old Testament literature."—*Guardian.*

Ecclesiastes; or, the Preacher.—" Of the Notes, it is sufficient to say that they are in every respect worthy of Dr PLUMPTRE's high reputation as a scholar and a critic, being at once learned, sensible, and practical.... An appendix, in which it is clearly proved that the author of *Ecclesiastes* anticipated Shakspeare and Tennyson in some of their finest thoughts and reflections, will be read with interest by students both of Hebrew and of English literature. Commentaries are seldom attractive reading. This little volume is a notable exception."—*The Scotsman.*

"In short, this little book is of far greater value than most of the larger and more elaborate commentaries on this Scripture. Indispensable to the scholar, it will render real and large help to all who have to expound the dramatic utterances of **The Preacher** whether in the Church or in the School."—*The Expositor.*

"The '*ideal* biography' of the author is one of the most exquisite and fascinating pieces of writing we have met with, and, granting its starting-point, throws wonderful light on many problems connected with the book. The notes illustrating the text are full of delicate criticism, fine glowing insight, and apt historical allusion. An abler volume than Professor PLUMPTRE's we could not desire."—*Baptist Magazine.*

Jeremiah, by A. W. STREANE. "The arrangement of the book is well treated on pp. xxx., 396, and the question of Baruch's relations with its composition on pp. xxvii., xxxiv., 317. The illustrations from English literature, history, monuments, works on botany, topography, etc., are good and plentiful, as indeed they are in other volumes of this series."—*Church Quarterly Review*, April, 1881.

"Mr STREANE'S **Jeremiah** consists of a series of admirable and well-nigh exhaustive notes on the text, with introduction and appendices, drawing the life, times, and character of the prophet, the style, contents, and arrangement of his prophecies, the traditions relating to Jeremiah, meant as a type of Christ (a most remarkable chapter), and other prophecies relating to Jeremiah."—*The English Churchman and Clerical Journal.*

Obadiah and Jonah. "This number of the admirable series of Scriptural expositions issued by the Syndics of the Cambridge University Press is well up to the mark. The numerous notes are excellent. No difficulty is shirked, and much light is thrown on the contents both of Obadiah and Jonah. Scholars and students of to-day are to be congratulated on having so large an amount of information on Biblical subjects, so clearly and ably put together, placed within their reach in such small bulk. To all Biblical students the series will be acceptable, and for the use of Sabbath-school teachers will prove invaluable."—*North British Daily Mail.*

"It is a very useful and sensible exposition of these two Minor Prophets, and deals very thoroughly and honestly with the immense difficulties of the later-named of the two, from the orthodox point of view."—*Expositor.*

"**Haggai and Zechariah.** This interesting little volume is of great value. It is one of the best books in that well-known series of scholarly and popular commentaries, 'the Cambridge Bible for Schools and Colleges' of which Dean Perowne is the General Editor. In the expositions of Archdeacon Perowne we are always sure to notice learning, ability, judgment and reverence.... The notes are terse and pointed, but full and reliable."—*Churchman.*

"**The Gospel according to St Matthew**, by the Rev. A. CARR. The introduction is able, scholarly, and eminently practical, as it bears on the authorship and contents of the Gospel, and the original form in which it is supposed to have been written. It is well illustrated by two excellent maps of the Holy Land and of the Sea of Galilee."—*English Churchman.*

"**St Matthew**, edited by A. CARR, M.A. **The Book of Joshua**, edited by G. F. MACLEAR, D.D. **The General Epistle of St James**, edited by E. H. PLUMPTRE, D.D. The introductions and notes are scholarly, and generally such as young readers need and can appreciate. The maps in both Joshua and Matthew are very good, and all matters of editing are faultless. Professor Plumptre's notes on 'The Epistle of St James' are models of terse, exact, and elegant renderings of the original, which is too often obscured in the authorised version."—*Nonconformist.*

"**St Mark**, with Notes by the Rev. G. F. MACLEAR, D.D. Into this small volume Dr Maclear, besides a clear and able Introduction to the Gospel, and the text of St Mark, has compressed many hundreds of valuable and helpful notes. In short, he has given us a capital manual of the kind required—containing all that is needed to illustrate the text, i.e. all that can be drawn from the history, geography, customs, and manners of the time. But as a handbook, giving in a clear and succinct form the information which a lad requires in order to stand an examination in the Gospel, it is admirable......I can very heartily commend it, not only to the senior boys and girls in our High Schools, but also to Sunday-school teachers, who may get from it the very kind of knowledge they often find it hardest to get."—*Expositor.*

OPINIONS OF THE PRESS.

"With the help of a book like this, an intelligent teacher may make 'Divinity' as interesting a lesson as any in the school course. The notes are of a kind that will be, for the most part, intelligible to boys of the lower forms of our public schools; but they may be read with greater profit by the fifth and sixth, in conjunction with the original text."—*The Academy.*

"**St Luke.** Canon FARRAR has supplied students of the Gospel with an admirable manual in this volume. It has all that copious variety of illustration, ingenuity of suggestion, and general soundness of interpretation which readers are accustomed to expect from the learned and eloquent editor. Any one who has been accustomed to associate the idea of 'dryness' with a commentary, should go to Canon Farrar's St Luke for a more correct impression. He will find that a commentary may be made interesting in the highest degree, and that without losing anything of its solid value. . . . But, so to speak, it is *too good* for some of the readers for whom it is intended."—*The Spectator.*

"Canon FARRAR's contribution to The Cambridge School Bible is one of the most valuable yet made. His annotations on **The Gospel according to St Luke**, while they display a scholarship at least as sound, and an erudition at least as wide and varied as those of the editors of St Matthew and St Mark, are rendered telling and attractive by a more lively imagination, a keener intellectual and spiritual insight, a more incisive and picturesque style. His *St Luke* is worthy to be ranked with Professor Plumptre's *St James*, than which no higher commendation can well be given."—*The Expositor.*

"**St Luke.** Edited by Canon FARRAR, D.D. We have received with pleasure this edition of the Gospel by St Luke, by Canon Farrar. It is another instalment of the best school commentary of the Bible we possess. Of the expository part of the work we cannot speak too highly. It is admirable in every way, and contains just the sort of information needed for Students of the English text unable to make use of the original Greek for themselves."—*The Nonconformist and Independent.*

"As a handbook to the third gospel, this small work is invaluable. The author has compressed into little space a vast mass of scholarly information. . . The notes are pithy, vigorous, and suggestive, abounding in pertinent illustrations from general literature, and aiding the youngest reader to an intelligent appreciation of the text. A finer contribution to 'The Cambridge Bible for Schools' has not yet been made."—*Baptist Magazine.*

"We were quite prepared to find in Canon FARRAR's **St Luke** a masterpiece of Biblical criticism and comment, and we are not disappointed by our examination of the volume before us. It reflects very faithfully the learning and critical insight of the Canon's greatest works, his 'Life of Christ' and his 'Life of St Paul', but differs widely from both in the terseness and condensation of its style. What Canon Farrar has evidently aimed at is to place before students as much information as possible within the limits of the smallest possible space, and in this aim he has hit the mark to perfection."—*The Examiner.*

The Gospel according to St John. "Of the notes we can say with confidence that they are useful, necessary, learned, and brief. To Divinity students, to teachers, and for private use, this compact Commentary will be found a valuable aid to the better understanding of the Sacred Text."—*School Guardian.*

"The new volume of the 'Cambridge Bible for Schools'—the **Gospel according to St John**, by the Rev. A. PLUMMER—shows as careful and thorough work as either of its predecessors. The introduction concisely yet fully describes the life of St John, the authenticity of the Gospel, its characteristics, its relation to the Synoptic Gospels, and to the Apostle's First Epistle, and the usual subjects referred to in an 'introduction'."—*The Christian Church.*

"The notes are extremely scholarly and valuable, and in most cases exhaustive, bringing to the elucidation of the text all that is best in commentaries, ancient and modern."—*The English Churchman and Clerical Journal.*

"(1) **The Acts of the Apostles.** By J. RAWSON LUMBY, D.D. (2) **The Second Epistle of the Corinthians**, edited by Professor LIAS. The introduction is pithy, and contains a mass of carefully-selected information on the authorship of the Acts, its designs, and its sources. ......The Second Epistle of the Corinthians is a manual beyond all praise, for the excellence of its pithy and pointed annotations, its analysis of the contents, and the fulness and value of its introduction."—*Examiner.*

"The concluding portion of the **Acts of the Apostles**, under the very competent editorship of Dr LUMBY, is a valuable addition to our school-books on that subject. Detailed criticism is impossible within the space at our command, but we may say that the ample notes touch with much exactness the very points on which most readers of the text desire information. Due reference is made, where necessary, to the Revised Version; the maps are excellent; and we do not know of any other volume where so much help is given to the complete understanding of one of the most important and, in many respects, difficult books of the New Testament."—*School Guardian.*

"The Rev. H. C. G. MOULE, M.A., has made a valuable addition to THE CAMBRIDGE BIBLE FOR SCHOOLS in his brief commentary on the **Epistle to the Romans**. The 'Notes' are very good, and lean, as the notes of a School Bible should, to the most commonly accepted and orthodox view of the inspired author's meaning; while the Introduction, and especially the Sketch of the Life of St Paul, is a model of condensation. It is as lively and pleasant to read as if two or three facts had not been crowded into well-nigh every sentence."—*Expositor.*

"**The Epistle to the Romans.** It is seldom we have met with a work so remarkable for the compression and condensation of all that is valuable in the smallest possible space as in the volume before us. Within its limited pages we have 'a sketch of the Life of St Paul,' we have further a critical account of the date of the Epistle to the Romans, of its language, and of its genuineness. The notes are numerous, full of matter, to the point, and leave no real difficulty or obscurity unexplained."—*The Examiner.*

"**The First Epistle to the Corinthians.** Edited by Professor LIAS. Every fresh instalment of this annotated edition of the Bible for Schools confirms the favourable opinion we formed of its value from the examination of its first number. The origin and plan of the Epistle are discussed with its character and genuineness."—*The Nonconformist.*

"**The Second Epistle to the Corinthians.** By Professor LIAS. **The General Epistles of St Peter and St Jude.** By E. H. PLUMPTRE, D.D. We welcome these additions to the valuable series of the Cambridge Bible. We have nothing to add to the commendation which we have from the first publication given to this edition of the Bible. It is enough to say that Professor Lias has completed his work on the two Epistles to the Corinthians in the same admirable manner as at first. Dr Plumptre has also completed the Catholic Epistles."—*Nonconformist.*

The Epistle to the Ephesians. By Rev. H. C. G. MOULE, M.A. "It seems to us the model of a School and College Commentary—comprehensive, but not cumbersome; scholarly, but not pedantic."—*Baptist Magazine.*

The Epistle to the Philippians. "There are few series more valued by theological students than 'The Cambridge Bible for Schools and Colleges,' and there will be no number of it more esteemed than that by Mr H. C. G. MOULE on the *Epistle to the Philippians.*"—*Record.*

"Another capital volume of 'The Cambridge Bible for Schools and Colleges.' The notes are a model of scholarly, lucid, and compact criticism."—*Baptist Magazine.*

Hebrews. "Like his (Canon Farrar's) commentary on Luke it possesses all the best characteristics of his writing. It is a work not only of an accomplished scholar, but of a skilled teacher."—*Baptist Magazine.*

"We heartily commend this volume of this excellent work."—*Sunday School Chronicle.*

"**The General Epistle of St James,** by Professor PLUMPTRE, D.D. Nevertheless it is, so far as I know, by far the best exposition of the Epistle of St James in the English language. Not Schoolboys or Students going in for an examination alone, but Ministers and Preachers of the Word, may get more real help from it than from the most costly and elaborate commentaries."—*Expositor.*

The Epistles of St John. By the Rev. A. PLUMMER, M.A., D.D. "This forms an admirable companion to the 'Commentary on the Gospel according to St John,' which was reviewed in *The Churchman* as soon as it appeared. Dr Plummer has some of the highest qualifications for such a task; and these two volumes, their size being considered, will bear comparison with the best Commentaries of the time."—*The Churchman.*

"Dr PLUMMER's edition of **the Epistles of St John** is worthy of its companions in the 'Cambridge Bible for Schools' Series. The subject, though not apparently extensive, is really one not easy to treat, and requiring to be treated at length, owing to the constant reference to obscure heresies in the Johannine writings. Dr Plummer has done his exegetical task well."—*The Saturday Review.*

THE CAMBRIDGE GREEK TESTAMENT
FOR SCHOOLS AND COLLEGES

With a Revised Text, based on the most recent critical authorities, and English Notes, prepared under the direction of the General Editor, THE VERY REVEREND J. J. S. PEROWNE, D.D.

"*Has achieved an excellence which puts it above criticism.*"—Expositor.

St Matthew. "Copious illustrations, gathered from a great variety of sources, make his notes a very valuable aid to the student. They are indeed remarkably interesting, while all explanations on meanings, applications, and the like are distinguished by their lucidity and good sense."—*Pall Mall Gazette.*

St Mark. "The Cambridge Greek Testament of which Dr MACLEAR'S edition of the Gospel according to St Mark is a volume, certainly supplies a want. Without pretending to compete with the leading commentaries, or to embody very much original research, it forms a most satisfactory introduction to the study of the New Testament in the original....Dr Maclear's introduction contains all that is known of St Mark's life; an account of the circumstances in which the Gospel was composed, with an estimate of the influence of St Peter's teaching upon St Mark; an excellent sketch of the special characteristics of this Gospel; an analysis, and a chapter on the text of the New Testament generally."—*Saturday Review.*

St Luke. "Of this second series we have a new volume by Archdeacon FARRAR on *St Luke*, completing the four Gospels....It gives us in clear and beautiful language the best results of modern scholarship. We have a most attractive *Introduction*. Then follows a sort of composite Greek text, representing fairly and in very beautiful type the consensus of modern textual critics. At the beginning of the exposition of each chapter of the Gospel are a few short critical notes giving the manuscript evidence for such various readings as seem to deserve mention. The expository notes are short, but clear and helpful. For young students and those who are not disposed to buy or to study the much more costly work of Godet, this seems to us to be the best book on the Greek Text of the Third Gospel."—*Methodist Recorder.*

St John. "We take this opportunity of recommending to ministers on probation, the very excellent volume of the same series on this part of the New Testament. We hope that most or all of our young ministers will prefer to study the volume in the *Cambridge Greek Testament for Schools.*"—*Methodist Recorder.*

The Acts of the Apostles. "Professor LUMBY has performed his laborious task well, and supplied us with a commentary the fulness and freshness of which Bible students will not be slow to appreciate. The volume is enriched with the usual copious indexes and four coloured maps."—*Glasgow Herald.*

I. Corinthians. "Mr LIAS is no novice in New Testament exposition, and the present series of essays and notes is an able and helpful addition to the existing books."—*Guardian.*

The Epistles of St John. "In the very useful and well annotated series of the Cambridge Greek Testament the volume on the Epistles of St John must hold a high position...The notes are brief, well informed and intelligent."—*Scotsman.*

CAMBRIDGE: PRINTED BY C. J. CLAY, M.A. AND SONS, AT THE UNIVERSITY PRESS.

CAMBRIDGE UNIVERSITY PRESS.

THE PITT PRESS SERIES.

⁎ *Many of the books in this list can be had in two volumes, Text and Notes separately.*

I. GREEK.

Aristophanes. Aves—Plutus—Ranæ. By W. C. GREEN, M.A., late Assistant Master at Rugby School. 3s. 6d. each.
Aristotle. Outlines of the Philosophy of. By EDWIN WALLACE, M.A., LL.D. Third Edition, Enlarged. 4s. 6d.
Euripides. Heracleidae. By E. A. BECK, M.A. 3s. 6d.
—— **Hercules Furens.** By A. GRAY, M.A., and J. T. HUTCHINSON, M.A. New Edit. 2s.
—— **Hippolytus.** By W. S. HADLEY, M.A. 2s.
—— **Iphigeneia in Aulis.** By C. E. S. HEADLAM, B.A. 2s. 6d.
Herodotus, Book V. By E. S. SHUCKBURGH, M.A. 3s.
—— **Book VI.** By the same Editor. 4s.
—— **Books VIII., IX.** By the same Editor. 4s. each.
—— **Book VIII. Ch. 1—90. Book IX. Ch. 1—89.** By the same Editor. 3s. 6d. each.
Homer. Odyssey, Books IX., X. By G. M. EDWARDS, M.A. 2s. 6d. each. BOOK XXI. By the same Editor. 2s.
—— **Iliad. Book XXII.** By the same Editor. 2s.
—— —— **Book XXIII.** By the same Editor. [*Nearly ready*.
Lucian. Somnium Charon Piscator et De Luctu. By W. E. HEITLAND, M.A., Fellow of St John's College, Cambridge. 3s. 6d.
—— **Menippus and Timon.** By E. C. MACKIE, M.A. [*Nearly ready*.
Platonis Apologia Socratis. By J. ADAM, M.A. 3s. 6d.
—— **Crito.** By the same Editor. 2s. 6d.
—— **Euthyphro.** By the same Editor. 2s. 6d.
Plutarch. Lives of the Gracchi. By Rev. H. A. HOLDEN, M.A., LL.D. 6s.
—— **Life of Nicias.** By the same Editor. 5s.
—— **Life of Sulla.** By the same Editor. 6s.
—— **Life of Timoleon.** By the same Editor. 6s.
Sophocles. Oedipus Tyrannus. School Edition. By R. C. JEBB, Litt.D., LL.D. 4s. 6d.
Thucydides. Book VII. By Rev. H. A. HOLDEN, M.A., LL.D. [*Nearly ready*.
Xenophon. Agesilaus. By H. HAILSTONE, M.A. 2s. 6d.
—— **Anabasis.** By A. PRETOR, M.A. Two vols. 7s. 6d.
—— **Books I. III. IV. and V.** By the same. 2s. each.
—— **Books II. VI. and VII.** By the same. 2s. 6d. each.
Xenophon. Cyropaedeia. Books I. II. By Rev. H. A. HOLDEN, M.A., LL.D. 2 vols. 6s.
—— —— **Books III. IV. and V.** By the same Editor. 5s.
—— —— **Books VI. VII. VIII.** By the same Editor. 5s.

London: Cambridge Warehouse, Ave Maria Lane.

50/12/90

II. LATIN.

Beda's Ecclesiastical History, Books III., IV. By J. E. B. MAYOR, M.A., and J. R. LUMBY, D.D. Revised Edition. 7s. 6d.

—— **Books I. II.** By the same Editors. [*In the Press.*

Caesar. De Bello Gallico, Comment. I. By A. G. PESKETT, M.A., Fellow of Magdalene College, Cambridge. 1s. 6d. COMMENT. II. III. 2s. COMMENT. I. II. III. 3s. COMMENT. IV. and V. 1s. 6d. COMMENT. VII. 2s. COMMENT. VI. and COMMENT. VIII. 1s. 6d. each.

—— **De Bello Civili, Comment. I.** By the same Editor. 3s.

Cicero. De Amicitia.—De Senectute. By J. S. REID, Litt.D., Fellow of Gonville and Caius College. 3s. 6d. each.

—— **In Gaium Verrem Actio Prima.** By H. COWIE, M.A. 1s. 6d.

—— **In Q. Caecilium Divinatio et in C. Verrem Actio.** By W. E. HEITLAND, M.A., and H. COWIE, M.A. 3s.

—— **Philippica Secunda.** By A. G. PESKETT, M.A. 3s. 6d.

—— **Oratio pro Archia Poeta.** By J. S. REID, Litt.D. 2s.

—— **Pro L. Cornelio Balbo Oratio.** By the same. 1s. 6d.

—— **Oratio pro Tito Annio Milone.** By JOHN SMYTH PURTON, B.D. 2s. 6d.

—— **Oratio pro L. Murena.** By W. E. HEITLAND, M.A. 3s.

—— **Pro Cn. Plancio Oratio,** by H. A. HOLDEN, LL.D. 4s. 6d.

—— **Pro P. Cornelio Sulla.** By J. S. REID, Litt.D. 3s. 6d.

—— **Somnium Scipionis.** By W. D. PEARMAN, M.A. 2s.

Horace. Epistles, Book I. By E. S. SHUCKBURGH, M.A., late Fellow of Emmanuel College. 2s. 6d.

Livy. Book IV. By H. M. STEPHENSON, M.A. 2s. 6d.

—— **Book V.** By L. WHIBLEY, M.A. 2s. 6d.

—— **Books XXI., XXII.** By M. S. DIMSDALE, M.A., Fellow of King's College. 2s. 6d. each.

—— **Book XXVII.** By Rev. H. M. STEPHENSON, M.A. 2s. 6d.

Lucan. Pharsaliae Liber Primus. By W. E. HEITLAND, M.A., and C. E. HASKINS, M.A. 1s. 6d.

Lucretius, Book V. By J. D. DUFF, M.A. 2s.

Ovidii Nasonis Fastorum Liber VI. By A. SIDGWICK, M.A., Tutor of Corpus Christi College, Oxford. 1s. 6d.

Quintus Curtius. A Portion of the History (Alexander in India). By W. E. HEITLAND, M.A., and T. E. RAVEN, B.A. With Two Maps. 3s. 6d.

Vergili Maronis Aeneidos Libri I.—XII. By A. SIDGWICK, M.A. 1s. 6d. each.

—— **Bucolica.** By the same Editor. 1s. 6d.

—— **Georgicon Libri I. II.** By the same Editor. 2s.

—— —— **Libri III. IV.** By the same Editor. 2s.

—— **The Complete Works.** By the same Editor. Two vols. Vol. I, containing the Introduction and Text. 3s. 6d. Vol. II. The Notes. 4s. 6d.

London: Cambridge Warehouse, Ave Maria Lane.

III. FRENCH.

Corneille. La Suite du Menteur. A Comedy in Five Acts.
By the late G. MASSON, B.A. 2s.

De Bonnechose. Lazare Hoche. By C. COLBECK, M.A.
Revised Edition. Four Maps. 2s.

D'Harleville. Le Vieux Célibataire. By G. MASSON, B.A. 2s.

De Lamartine. Jeanne D'Arc. By Rev. A. C. CLAPIN,
M.A. New edition revised, by A. R. ROPES, M.A. 1s. 6d.

De Vigny. La Canne de Jonc. By Rev. H. A. BULL,
M.A., late Master at Wellington College. 2s.

Erckmann-Chatrian. La Guerre. By Rev. A. C. CLAPIN,
M.A. 3s.

La Baronne de Staël-Holstein. Le Directoire. (Considérations sur la Révolution Française. Troisième et quatrième parties.) Revised and enlarged. By G. MASSON, B.A., and G. W. PROTHERO, M.A. 2s.

—————— **Dix Années d'Exil. Livre II. Chapitres 1—8.**
By the same Editors. New Edition, enlarged. 2s.

Lemercier. Fredegonde et Brunehaut. A Tragedy in Five
Acts. By GUSTAVE MASSON, B.A. 2s.

Molière. Le Bourgeois Gentilhomme, Comédie-Ballet en
Cinq Actes. (1670.) By Rev. A. C. CLAPIN, M.A. Revised Edition. 1s. 6d.

—————— **L'École des Femmes.** By G. SAINTSBURY, M.A. 2s. 6d.

—————— **Les Précieuses Ridicules.** By E. G. W. BRAUNHOLTZ,
M.A., Ph.D. 2s.

—————— —————— **Abridged Edition.** 1s.

Piron. La Métromanie. A Comedy. By G. MASSON, B.A. 2s.

Racine. Les Plaideurs. By E. G. W. BRAUNHOLTZ, M.A. 2s.

—————— —————— **Abridged Edition.** 1s.

Sainte-Beuve. M. Daru (Causeries du Lundi, Vol. IX.).
By G. MASSON, B.A. 2s.

Saintine. Picciola. By Rev. A. C. CLAPIN, M.A. 2s.

Scribe and Legouvé. Bataille de Dames. By Rev. H. A.
BULL, M.A. 2s.

Scribe. Le Verre d'Eau. By C. COLBECK, M.A. 2s.

Sédaine. Le Philosophe sans le savoir. By Rev. H. A.
BULL, M.A. 2s.

Thierry. Lettres sur l'histoire de France (XIII.—XXIV.).
By G. MASSON, B.A., and G. W. PROTHERO, M.A. 2s. 6d.

—————— **Récits des Temps Mérovingiens I.—III.** By GUSTAVE
MASSON, B.A. Univ. Gallic., and A. R. ROPES, M.A. With Map. 3s.

Villemain. Lascaris ou Les Grecs du XVe Siècle, Nouvelle
Historique. By G. MASSON, B.A. 2s.

Voltaire. Histoire du Siècle de Louis XIV. Chaps. I.—
XIII. By G. MASSON, B.A., and G. W. PROTHERO, M.A. 2s. 6d. PART II.
CHAPS. XIV.—XXIV. 2s. 6d. PART III. CHAPS. XXV. to end. 2s. 6d.

Xavier de Maistre. La Jeune Sibérienne. Le Lépreux de
la Cité D'Aoste. By G. MASSON, B.A. 1s. 6d.

London: Cambridge Warehouse, Ave Maria Lane.

IV. GERMAN.

Ballads on German History. By W. WAGNER, Ph.D. 2s.

Benedix. Doctor Wespe. Lustspiel in fünf Aufzügen. By KARL HERMANN BREUL, M.A., Ph.D. 3s.

Freytag. Der Staat Friedrichs des Grossen. By WILHELM WAGNER, Ph.D. 2s.

German Dactylic Poetry. By WILHELM WAGNER, Ph.D. 3s.

Goethe's Knabenjahre. (1749—1759.) By W. WAGNER, Ph.D. New edition revised and enlarged, by J. W. CARTMELL, M.A. 2s.

—— **Hermann und Dorothea.** By WILHELM WAGNER, Ph.D. New edition revised, by J. W. CARTMELL, M.A. 3s. 6d.

Gutzkow. Zopf und Schwert. Lustspiel in fünf Aufzügen. By H. J. WOLSTENHOLME, B.A. (Lond.). 3s. 6d.

Hauff. Das Bild des Kaisers. By KARL HERMANN BREUL, M.A., Ph.D., University Lecturer in German. 3s.

—— **Das Wirthshaus im Spessart.** By A. SCHLOTTMANN, Ph.D. 3s. 6d.

—— **Die Karavane.** By A. SCHLOTTMANN, Ph.D. 3s. 6d.

Immermann. Der Oberhof. A Tale of Westphalian Life, by WILHELM WAGNER, Ph.D. 3s.

Kohlrausch. Das Jahr 1813. By WILHELM WAGNER, Ph.D. 2s.

Lessing and Gellert. Selected Fables. By KARL HERMANN BREUL, M.A., Ph.D. 3s.

Mendelssohn's Letters. Selections from. By J. SIME, M.A. 3s.

Raumer. Der erste Kreuzzug (1095—1099). By WILHELM WAGNER, Ph.D. 2s.

Riehl. Culturgeschichtliche Novellen. By H. J. WOLSTENHOLME, B.A. (Lond.). 3s. 6d.

Schiller. Wilhelm Tell. By KARL HERMANN BREUL, M.A., Ph.D. 2s. 6d.

—————— **Abridged Edition.** 1s. 6d.

Uhland. Ernst, Herzog von Schwaben. By H. J. WOLSTENHOLME, B.A. 3s. 6d.

V. ENGLISH.

Ancient Philosophy from Thales to Cicero, A Sketch of. By JOSEPH B. MAYOR, M.A. 3s. 6d.

An Apologie for Poetrie by Sir PHILIP SIDNEY. By E. S. SHUCKBURGH, M.A. The Text is a revision of that of the first edition of 1595. 3s.

Bacon's History of the Reign of King Henry VII. By the Rev. Professor LUMBY, D.D. 3s.

Cowley's Essays. By the Rev. Professor LUMBY, D.D. 4s.

London: Cambridge Warehouse, Ave Maria Lane.

Milton's Comus and Arcades. By A. W. VERITY, M.A., sometime Scholar of Trinity College. 3s.
More's History of King Richard III. By J. RAWSON LUMBY, D.D. 3s. 6d.
More's Utopia. By Rev. Prof. LUMBY, D.D. 3s. 6d.
The Two Noble Kinsmen. By the Rev. Professor SKEAT, Litt.D. 3s. 6d.

VI. EDUCATIONAL SCIENCE.

Comenius, John Amos. Bishop of the Moravians. His Life and Educational Works, by S. S. LAURIE, A.M., F.R.S.E. 3s. 6d.
Education, Three Lectures on the Practice of. I. On Marking, by H. W. EVE, M.A. II. On Stimulus, by A. SIDGWICK, M.A. III. On the Teaching of Latin Verse Composition, by E. A. ABBOTT, D.D. 2s.
Stimulus. A Lecture delivered for the Teachers' Training Syndicate, May, 1882, by A. SIDGWICK, M.A. 1s.
Locke on Education. By the Rev. R. H. QUICK, M.A. 3s. 6d.
Milton's Tractate on Education. A facsimile reprint from the Edition of 1673. By O. BROWNING, M.A. 2s.
Modern Languages, Lectures on the Teaching of. By C. COLBECK, M.A. 2s.
Teacher, General Aims of the, and Form Management. Two Lectures delivered in the University of Cambridge in the Lent Term, 1883, by F. W. FARRAR, D.D., and R. B. POOLE, B.D. 1s. 6d.
Teaching, Theory and Practice of. By the Rev. E. THRING, M.A., late Head Master of Uppingham School. New Edition. 4s. 6d.

British India, a Short History of. By E. S. CARLOS, M.A., late Head Master of Exeter Grammar School. 1s.
Geography, Elementary Commercial. A Sketch of the Commodities and the Countries of the World. By H. R. MILL, D.Sc., F.R.S.E. 1s.
Geography, an Atlas of Commercial. (A Companion to the above.) By J. G. BARTHOLOMEW, F.R.G.S. With an Introduction by HUGH ROBERT MILL, D.Sc. 3s.

VII. MATHEMATICS.

Euclid's Elements of Geometry. Books I. and II. By H. M. TAYLOR, M.A., Fellow and late Tutor of Trinity College, Cambridge. 1s. 6d.
———— ———— Books III. and IV. By the same Editor. 1s. 6d.
———— ———— Books I.—IV., in one Volume. 3s.
Elementary Algebra (with Answers to the Examples). By W. W. ROUSE BALL, M.A. 4s. 6d.
Elements of Statics. By S. L. LONEY, M.A. 5s.
Elements of Dynamics. By the same Editor. [*Nearly ready.*
Other Volumes are in preparation.

London: Cambridge Warehouse, Ave Maria Lane.

The Cambridge Bible for Schools and Colleges.

GENERAL EDITOR: J. J. S. PEROWNE, D.D.,
BISHOP OF WORCESTER.

"*It is difficult to commend too highly this excellent series.*—Guardian.

"*The modesty of the general title of this series has, we believe, led many to misunderstand its character and underrate its value. The books are well suited for study in the upper forms of our best schools, but not the less are they adapted to the wants of all Bible students who are not specialists. We doubt, indeed, whether any of the numerous popular commentaries recently issued in this country will be found more serviceable for general use.*"—Academy.

Now Ready. Cloth, Extra Fcap. 8vo. With Maps.

Book of Joshua. By Rev. G. F. MACLEAR, D.D. 2s. 6d.
Book of Judges. By Rev. J. J. LIAS, M.A. 3s. 6d.
First Book of Samuel. By Rev. Prof. KIRKPATRICK, B.D. 3s. 6d.
Second Book of Samuel. By the same Editor. 3s. 6d.
First Book of Kings. By Rev. Prof. LUMBY, D.D. 3s. 6d.
Second Book of Kings. By Rev. Prof. LUMBY, D.D. 3s. 6d.
Book of Job. By Rev. A. B. DAVIDSON, D.D. 5s.
Book of Ecclesiastes. By Very Rev. E. H. PLUMPTRE, D.D. 5s.
Book of Jeremiah. By Rev. A. W. STREANE, M.A. 4s. 6d.
Book of Hosea. By Rev. T. K. CHEYNE, M.A., D.D. 3s.
Books of Obadiah & Jonah. By Archdeacon PEROWNE. 2s. 6d.
Book of Micah. By Rev. T. K. CHEYNE, M.A., D.D. 1s. 6d.
Haggai, Zechariah & Malachi. By Arch. PEROWNE. 3s. 6d.
Book of Malachi. By Archdeacon PEROWNE. 1s.
Gospel according to St Matthew. By Rev. A. CARR, M.A. 2s. 6d.
Gospel according to St Mark. By Rev. G. F. MACLEAR, D.D. 2s. 6d.
Gospel according to St Luke. By Arch. FARRAR, D.D. 4s. 6d.
Gospel according to St John. By Rev. A. PLUMMER, D.D. 4s. 6d.
Acts of the Apostles. By Rev. Prof. LUMBY, D.D. 4s. 6d.
Epistle to the Romans. By Rev. H. C. G. MOULE, M.A. 3s. 6d.
First Corinthians. By Rev. J. J. LIAS, M.A. With Map. 2s.
Second Corinthians. By Rev. J. J. LIAS, M.A. With Map. 2s.
Epistle to the Galatians. By Rev. E. H. PEROWNE, D.D. 1s. 6d.

London: Cambridge Warehouse, Ave Maria Lane.

Epistle to the Ephesians. By Rev. H. C. G. MOULE, M.A. 2s. 6d.
Epistle to the Philippians. By the same Editor. 2s. 6d.
Epistles to the Thessalonians. By Rev. G. G. FINDLAY, M.A. 2s.
Epistle to the Hebrews. By Arch. FARRAR, D.D. 3s. 6d.
General Epistle of St James. By Very Rev. E. H. PLUMPTRE, D.D. 1s. 6d.
Epistles of St Peter and St Jude. By Very Rev. E. H. PLUMPTRE, D.D. 2s. 6d.
Epistles of St John. By Rev. A. PLUMMER, M.A., D.D. 3s. 6d.
Book of Revelation. By Rev. W. H. SIMCOX, M.A. 3s.

Preparing.

Book of Genesis. By the BISHOP OF WORCESTER.
Books of Exodus, Numbers and Deuteronomy. By Rev. C. D. GINSBURG, LL.D.
Books of Ezra and Nehemiah. By Rev. Prof. RYLE, M.A.
Book of Psalms. Part I. By Rev. Prof. KIRKPATRICK, B.D.
Book of Isaiah. By Prof. W. ROBERTSON SMITH, M.A.
Book of Ezekiel. By Rev. A. B. DAVIDSON, D.D.
Epistles to the Colossians and Philemon. By Rev. H. C. G. MOULE, M.A.
Epistles to Timothy & Titus. By Rev. A. E. HUMPHREYS, M.A.

The Smaller Cambridge Bible for Schools.

The Smaller Cambridge Bible for Schools will form an entirely new series of commentaries on some selected books of the Bible. It is expected that they will be prepared for the most part by the Editors of the larger series (The Cambridge Bible for Schools and Colleges). The volumes will be issued at a low price, and will be suitable to the requirements of preparatory and elementary schools.

Now ready.
First and Second Books of Samuel. By Rev. Prof. KIRKPATRICK, B.D. 1s. each.
First Book of Kings. By Rev. Prof. LUMBY, D.D. 1s.
Gospel according to St Matthew. By Rev. A. CARR, M.A. 1s.
Gospel according to St Mark. By Rev. G. F. MACLEAR, D.D. 1s.
Gospel according to St Luke. By Archdeacon FARRAR. 1s.
Acts of the Apostles. By Rev. Prof. LUMBY, D.D. 1s.

Nearly ready.
Second Book of Kings. By Rev. Prof. LUMBY, D.D.
Gospel according to St John. By Rev. A. PLUMMER, D.D.

London: Cambridge Warehouse, Ave Maria Lane.

The Cambridge Greek Testament for Schools and Colleges,

with a Revised Text, based on the most recent critical authorities, and English Notes, prepared under the direction of the

GENERAL EDITOR, J. J. S. PEROWNE, D.D.,
BISHOP OF WORCESTER.

Gospel according to St Matthew. By Rev. A. CARR, M.A.
With 4 Maps. 4s. 6d.

Gospel according to St Mark. By Rev. G. F. MACLEAR, D.D.
With 3 Maps. 4s. 6d.

Gospel according to St Luke. By Archdeacon FARRAR.
With 4 Maps. 6s.

Gospel according to St John. By Rev. A. PLUMMER, D.D.
With 4 Maps. 6s.

Acts of the Apostles. By Rev. Professor LUMBY, D.D.
With 4 Maps. 6s.

First Epistle to the Corinthians. By Rev. J. J. LIAS, M.A. 3s.

Second Epistle to the Corinthians. By Rev. J. J. LIAS, M.A.
[*In the Press.*

Epistle to the Hebrews. By Archdeacon FARRAR, D.D. 3s. 6d.

Epistle of St James. By Very Rev. E. H. PLUMPTRE, D.D.
[*Preparing.*

Epistles of St John. By Rev. A. PLUMMER, M.A., D.D. 4s.

London: C. J. CLAY AND SONS,
CAMBRIDGE WAREHOUSE, AVE MARIA LANE.
Glasgow: 263, ARGYLE STREET.
Cambridge: DEIGHTON, BELL AND CO.
Leipzig: F. A. BROCKHAUS.
New York: MACMILLAN AND CO.

www.ingramcontent.com/pod-product-compliance
Lightning Source LLC
Chambersburg PA
CBHW020121170426
43199CB00009B/583